Studies in Female Sexuality

FORUM STUDIES IN SEXUAL BEHAVIOUR

SANDRA McDERMOTT

Studies in Female Sexuality

THE ODYSSEY PRESS
London

© The Odyssey Press 1970
Published by The Odyssey Press Ltd,
2 Bramber Road,
West Kensington, W.14
A division of Penthouse International

Set by Computaset Ltd,
printed in Great Britain by
Anchor Press Ltd.,
and bound by
Wm. Brendon & Son Ltd, both of Tiptree, Essex.

SBN 850 95080 5

Contents

Preface

This is the second in a series of volumes — of which *The Outer Fringe of Sex* by Maurice North, was the first — in the *Forum Studies in Sexual Behaviour.* The purpose of this series is to expand, through the research facilities of the British monthly magazine, *Forum*, the general knowledge of contemporary sexual behaviour in Great Britain in all its aspects.

Studies in Female Sexuality is based on an analysis of *Forum's* two-year study among British women of varying ages, backgrounds and educational levels. They assisted us freely — to the surprise of a number of people in the medical and allied professions — not only because they themselves stood to gain considerably from the insight resulting from their interviews (each undertaking a three to four hour recall), but also because many of them clearly wanted to do something about the widespread male ignorance regarding women's sexuality. We feel that this volume may now help to dispel many such misconceptions.

Albert Z. Freedman
Editor, *Forum.*

Introduction

In 1929 Wilhelm Reich wrote in *The Sexual Revolution* (reissue, London, 1952): 'A few years ago the idea that a girl of fifteen or sixteen — though she may be sexually mature — could have a boyfriend seemed absurd; today it has already become a matter for serious discussion; in a few more years it will be as much a matter of course as it is today the right of the unmarried female to have a sexual partner. A hundred years from now, such demands as that woman teachers should have no sex-life will provoke the same incredulous smiles as does today mention of the times when men put chastity belts on their women. Just as ridiculous will appear what today is almost general ideology: that the man has to seduce a woman, while a woman is not supposed to seduce a man.'

In some ways things have moved a little faster than Reich prophesied. The demand that a woman teacher should have no sex-life has provoked 'incredulous smiles' for some time now, but the seduction of men by women is not yet part of the *status quo*. The origins of such belief are almost primeval: man the hunter, woman the hunted. It might now be accepted that in conditions of privacy, women do make initial approaches, but within the general context of sexual relationships, few men are prepared to be pursued.

Such definition of roles, and the unspoken rules of feminine behaviour, are evidence that the differences between men and women are the result of complex psychological, social, economic and environmental factors. That is not to say that female behaviour has not and will not change. As we have already seen, three decades have witnessed a minor revolution in contrast to progress in the preceding century. As the factors which determine behaviour change, so does behaviour itself.

Thus we come to the purpose of this book, which is an attempt to provide a picture of the changes taking place and the way in which women are adapting their behaviour in a changing sexual environment. Through a series of interviews undertaken over the last two years we have been able to penetrate the thoughts, feelings, philosophies and motivations of women of many ages: for when a woman talks of her sexuality she is speaking of the most influential aspect of her existence.

Today, although we consider our society permissive, we still fall into the trap of considering sex and sexuality as things apart from everyday life. One of the main aims of this book is to show that sexuality is an integral part of the personality. Thus, women who consider their sexuality as another chamber of their being, the door which can be opened and shut at will, will never be able to accept themselves fully as complete individuals.

There is more to female sexuality than the ability to attract a man and please him in bed; there is more to sexual experience than the physical act of love-making. And so it is that the sexuality of a woman has more than a little influence on the qualities of her personality, whether she is likeable, disagreeable, warm, attractive, sensitive to others, mean or generous. Her sexual experience influences her environment, her financial position, her emotional state, and, perhaps, the number of children she has.

Women tend to go where men take them. If a husband lands a job which means moving to another continent then in all probability his wife will go too. If a woman, who has a sexual relationship and children with a man who refuses to work, wants to stay with him at all costs, then she too will be poor. One woman I interviewed was living alone in a tiny, lonely London bedsitter solely because of a disastrous sexual relationship with her husband.

If it is difficult for women to assert themselves truly, it is because they are deeply aware of what men think women *ought* to be, which, for the most part, clashes with their need for masculine attention. Some women spend so much time in trying to keep up with the masculine ideal of femininity that they lose all sight of their real selves and life becomes a struggle to perpetuate their own myth. Every one of the women interviewed felt that only a minority of men they had ever encountered had been fully aware of feminine psychological and physical needs. Men, it might be said, will not let women be what they really are.

However, the potential strength of most women is enormous. They are capable of great endurance, so much so that it may be taken for weakness and an inability to alter their situation. Recent experiments in America with control groups of baby boys and girls showed that, when shown photographs of people, more reaction was obtained from the baby girls. The boys were more interested when shown things. Simple observation proves that after the ending of a highly emotional relationship a woman will immediately seek another similar relationship, while men seem to find it easier to absorb themselves in achievements, in their work or interests. It is also true that most women do not achieve the same security as men from the realisation of material and intellectual needs. Men are capable of obtaining security from the knowledge that their desire for books, cars, friends, food etc. are being met. The same men may also desire a woman as part of their security and happiness, but infrequently regard her as the magic spell which will ensure satisfaction of all their desires, which is the way women tend to view the man in their life.

Recent innovations, such as the Pill, and the realisation that it is now possible for more women to be economically independent, are helping in some degree to release women from their reliance upon men. Single girls in particular are no longer forced into marriage because they are tired of penny-pinching on meagre wages. They can afford their own flats and, as Virginia Woolf perceived and revealed in her writing, the ability of women to live alone in comfort is of tremendous significance.

We are now at a time when, in certain directions, women are liberated and emancipated, while in other ways attitudes remain which have prevailed since time immemorial. Thus conflict within the individual woman is bound to arise. She is forced into making decisions she has never had to make previously. For instance, she must often make the choice between motherhood and career, between the economic freedom of the single girl and the financial reliance on a man in marriage, between virginity and sexual experience before marriage. The opportunity to choose in these matters has never before so clearly presented itself.

What a woman decides is to a great extent determined by her upbringing and her emotional state at the time, but gradually the responsibility of making decisions falls on her own shoulders. During the course of the interviews it became obvious that the younger woman, of under twenty-five or less, is more aware of her individual autonomy. Whether this be a realisation on her part or whether it has been brought about through the rejection of preconceived values is hard to say.

It was quite remarkable that the women who took part in this study were immediately so open and completely honest. I met with no reluctance to discuss any point. Those whose sex life was unsatisfactory were willing to say so without any feeling that they were damaging their own pride. It seems that the bragging woman does not exist in the same way as 'the bragging man' who entertains the public bar with stories of his sexual exploits, perhaps returning home that same night to his usual lonely masturbation and fantasies. It was refreshing to learn that women, so long considered the most repressed of the two sexes, did not find it necessary to lie in order to impress me, another woman. It would appear that women do not necessarily equate their sexual capacities and performance with proof of their femininity, in the same way that men equate such with virility and masculinity. The reader might automatically infer that any woman who offered to be interviewed in this way was by nature an exhibitionist. While there is no doubt that there is an element of the exhibitionist in most women, I would state emphatically that at no time did I suspect that this was an underlying motive for undertaking the interview.

Subjects were found through various means. Advertisements were placed in various publications but the great bulk of response came from the thousands of subscribers to the British monthly periodical, *Forum*. Many women were ready to volunteer because their own experiences had led them to believe that there were far too many false notions concerning the nature of female sexuality. Only one woman in all said that she had agreed to be interviewed for 'a bit of a giggle'.

An interesting point was that some found the interview therapeutic. One woman decided that looking at her life in retrospect was so beneficial to her that she wrote to me later to let me know that she had decided to keep a diary. Another girl found that talking so frankly, after having kept her thoughts to herself for so long, renewed her ability to communicate. Two weeks later she telephoned to say that she had moved out of her isolated room and had found a job in a hotel which would involve contact with large numbers of people, as well as more personal relationships with other members of the staff. The majority of the interviewers took place in the subject's own home where they were able to relax in a familiar environment. The married women had invariably told their husbands about the interview; in one case I interviewed a thirty-one-year-old woman with the man she lived with present.

No general technique of approach was employed except the attempt to be as honest and straightforward with the subject as I hoped they would be with me. I felt instinctively that a clinical attitude would have been disastrous. I found that if the interviewee felt I had a genuine interest in her as a person, rather than an anonymous computer, her response was both fuller and more spontaneous. This approach entailed sharing jokes and exchanging anecdotes and experiences to the extent that the conversation often exceeded the capacity of the tape.

1 Fantasy and Reality

One does not have to be a student of psychology to realise that all children are fascinated by themselves and the fact of their own existence. It is a natural consequence that the little girl wants to know about her origins; her body is her most prized possession – she is proud of everything it produces, including the excreta which we, as conditioned adults, appear to find so distasteful. She is surprised and curious about the pleasant sensations she feels when exploring her genitals. She begins to notice that her own body is unlike her mother's, and even more unlike her father's. In her innocence she dares to ask questions.

In most cases incidents of questioning on sexual matters at this age are beyond memory, but many of the women interviewed spoke of the impression they gained that their parents were reluctant to discuss sex. Through this they came to the conclusion that if discussion of sex was taboo then sex must be either dangerous, dirty or completely incomprehensible. Thus an unmistakable basis for guilt was created through the stony silence of parents, the hurried changing of the subject, and the frantic covering of bodies when daughters inadvertently caught their parents in a state of undress. The non-verbal method of warning children off the subject of sex is as strong as if the parent were to tell the child that sex is evil. Children are immensely sensitive to implications, and perceptive enough to recognise even the most subtle diversions. Consequently, they sometimes begin to fear sex as much as they fear spooks in the night. Frequently this fear is carried into adulthood.

Said fifty-one-year-old Mary: 'My parents never talked to me about sex. I didn't even learn about menstruation from my mother. I was thirteen when I had my first period. I discovered it in the toilet at school; I must admit that I was rather frightened. I never told anyone, not even my mother. I felt that it was something you just didn't talk about'.

Not one word had passed between this girl and her mother on the subject of sex and this fact alone had led her to believe that sex was so frightening as to be unmentionable. Her parents were poor and quarrelled often. As she grew older she realised that most of their arguments concerned sex: 'My mother would nag my father about us being poor and when she was angry she would cut off his ration'. She admits that when she married at the age of twenty-one both she and her husband were abysmally ignorant: 'The terrible tragedy was that my husband and I were both reasonably intelligent people and yet we did not know the rudiments of sex'. During the early stages of their marriage they used condoms as a contraceptive method. However, two pregnancies resulted. Mary lost all faith in this contraceptive method. She and her husband could not afford to have more children. Their knowledge of contraception went no further than condoms and so they resorted to coitus interruptus. The effect on Mary, both physically and psychologically, was disastrous and eventually she had a nervous breakdown. That was sixteen years ago, but since then she had been unable to reach orgasm and suffers from insomnia and claustrophobia: 'Sex for me is not distasteful, but I know that it is not complete'.

It is true that Mary could have sought contraceptive advice on making the discovery that condoms were not adequate, but her upbringing had taught her to believe that sex 'just wasn't something you talked about'. Faint wonder that it never entered her head to discuss contraception with a total stranger. After her breakdown she was advised by doctors to use the cap as a contraceptive device – but that was thirty years too late.

Throughout the interviews there was evidence of parents who had absolutely refused to mention sex. Looking back across the years, which had held a disastrous marriage, twenty-three-year-old June told me: 'My parents never talked about sex at all. I don't think that it was because they considered it dirty but as far as they were concerned it didn't exist, at least when it came to talking about it'. When parents refuse to discuss sex, or tell their children ridiculous stories about delivery via storks, it is inevitable that the child will begin to apply words such as 'rude' and 'naughty' to the sexual organs. The little girl soon realises that matters relating to the genital areas are socially unacceptable and that she can attract a good deal of attention by taking down her knickers in front of visitors. In this way, an astute child will often use this kind of display and the ability to embarrass her parents, as a weapon for family power politics.

In this direction the interviews reflected little difference between those who described their backgrounds as working class and those who described their backgrounds as middle class. The only child seems to suffer more than the child with siblings of a smiliar age group: totally isolated from the sight of fellow children at bathtime and bedtime, the only child sometimes has a more traumatic experience on discovering the difference between herself and boys. An only child may also have the urge to change her sex on discovering differentiation. 'It never occurred to me that there was any difference between the sexes apart from dress', remarked twenty-year-old Sue. 'When I discovered that boys urinated standing up I badly wanted to be able to do this and tried to emmulate them, but I was scared stiff that my parents would catch me'.

Those who spent their early childhood in the country probably had the most balanced sex education of all. They were introduced to sex through the animal world. It is also true that those who live close to nature are able to sense that sex is at the same time both commonplace and magical: 'I can't remember a time when I didn't know the crude facts of life, because my father kept the parish bull . . . ', and 'I knew about sex when I was six years old. We lived in the country and when the animals gave birth it was explained to me that this was how human children were born. I was also allowed to see cows being served'.

In view of the fact that the two women quoted above, as well as others with similar stories, have never encountered any major sexual problem, I would suggest that many of the city-bred women interviewed would probably have had a far happier adolescence and mature sex life if their parents had possessed enough basic common sense to have bought their daughters a pair of rabbits and let them watch. However, what is learnt from observing animals must also be qualified by parents, as is illustrated by the following: 'I lived on a farm, so I knew all about animal procreation from as far back as I can remember. It wasn't until I was older that I thought this might apply to people. My parents told me about sex but I never understood it. For example, I asked my mother how to tell the difference between boys and girls and she said that it was the same as the difference between dog and bitch puppies. I saw animals mating and my mother said that that was the way it was with people. I couldn't work it out at all. I could only relate it to animals'.

It is not only the guilt caused by ignorance and false morality which

3

leads to such confusion and turbulence, there is also much fear — fear of domination, of penetration and of child-birth. 'At the age of sixteen I knew nothing about sex. I thought that babies were born through the mother having her stomach ripped open. I used to have pleasant feelings when boys touched my breasts, but if they went any further I used to get frightened and ended up wrestling with them. I didn't really know what they were after', commented Edna, who was forty-seven. For Liza the fright was similar: 'When I first found out about sex through reading books I was horrified. I couldn't imagine how a baby could get through such a small space'. Ruth, twenty, and a confirmed lesbian, remarked: 'I picked up most of my information from the girls at school. It was like piecing together a jig-saw from bits of dirty jokes. When I finally understood I was revolted by the whole idea that a man could do *that* to me. I just couldn't ever see myself doing it'.

The stubborn refusal on the part of parents to answer simple questions breeds deep insecurity within the child. One girl was so convinced of her parents' total ignorance concerning sex that she developed an obsession that she was adopted: 'I must have been a particularly stupid child because until I was about eight years old it never even occurred to me that there was some kind of conspiracy afoot to prevent me from knowing certain things. I woke up to this when other children began to shake my faith in the story of the stork. I don't know that I ever believed that story, but it didn't seem too important one way or the other, until I could no longer accept it at all. Then all of a sudden it became tremendously important to me to know where I came from. My questions were answered with more stork tales, or else mutterings about gooseberry bushes. I knew all this wasn't true and went through a stage when I thought that my parents actually believed it. I was worried that I knew something which they didn't. I thought that they really had found me under a gooseberry bush and adopted me. I went through this period thinking that I was adopted and not knowing whether to tell my parents that babies really didn't just grow under bushes. I think that if I had actually known at the time where babies did come from I would have gone to my parents with a view to telling them something I thought they didn't know'.

In many cases it was true that even if parents had been able to overcome their embarrassment, their own knowledge of the reproductive system was insufficient for them to have explained satisfactorily. A twenty-three-year-old from Yorkshire had felt this: 'Maybe my parents just assumed that I knew all about sex because they never mentioned it. They were embarrassed about it and weren't capable of explaining it to me. I don't think that they even knew what actually caused something like menstruation'. It is hardly surprising that this girl became pregnant at seventeen, and was forced into a tragic marriage because of worry about what the neighbours might think. Eventually, she finished up answering 'lonely hearts' advertisements and having sex with every man she met. At the time of the interview she was quite unable to understand why none of these men ever took her out more than once.

Insecurity arises because the child feels that if her parents are unable to talk about sex they are unable to cope with sex. Serious imbalances are caused by daughters over-hearing their parents arguing about sex, or mothers whispering loudly, 'not in front of the children', whenever her husband makes advances. Thus the child equates the idea of love-making with furtiveness and secrecy. This is emphasised in adolescence when initial sexual experiences are carried out in back alleys. Many women find that sex within the socially accepted confines of marriage lacks excitement because the ingredient of 'the forbidden' is removed. Also during adolescence many of the women were given warnings, although what they were supposed to be afraid of was rarely referred to. Perhaps the most obvious example of terror for terror's sake cropped up in an interview where the woman said: 'They told me to be careful but they never said what it was I had to be careful about'. One woman interviewed had so strongly sensed her parents' sexual problems as a child that she rejected any idea that they might be able to inform her. 'I never talked to my parents about sex, as I knew that my mother didn't like sexual matters. Whenever she started to tell me about sex I would tell her to stop because instinctively I felt that her attitude to sex was wrong, as I have always felt that sex was a tremendously good force. Consequently, I knew very little about the biological aspects of sex until I made love at the age of seventeen'. Although, the relationship with her mother obviously suffered because of the child's realisation of her mother's attitude, she probably saved herself even more confusion – such as that experienced by twenty-four-year-old Marilyn. Her experience was: 'My parents never mentioned sex. They made me feel very guilty about it all and I was never allowed to undress in front of them. When I started going out with boys my mother would say – "Don't get up to anything" – although, she never explained what "anything" was.

'I came home from school once and asked her what "fuck" meant, as I had just heard the word. She didn't tell me what it meant, but she did tell my father about the incident when he came home, and he gave me a good thrashing, again without telling me what the word meant. When I

5

eventually found out about sex I was rather frightened. I think that this had something to do with me being intimidated by men, which is why I always give in. This is because of my father. He was so aggressive and I always think that if men don't get what they want they will resort to violence as he did'.

Even parents who brought themselves to discuss sex with their daughter, managed to communicate a sense of worry. As with the mother of this twenty-one-year-old laboratory technician: 'When I began at my secondary school, I was very green. By the time I left, I thought that I was in possession of all the facts. This wasn't quite true but I did have a grasp of the basic facts about sex. My mother tried to talk to me about it, but looking back, I can see it was difficult for her and she found it embarrassing. She explained as much as she could, placing the emphasis upon the awful consequences of intercourse — unwanted and deserted babies, abortion and V.D. I don't think that she deliberately set out to frighten me; she just told me the way things appeared to her'.

Sexual pleasure in the sense of passion and abandon does not exist for children. Small girls may obtain pleasant sensations from touching their own genitals or through having their genitals explored by other children, but they are generally motivated more by curiosity. Most of the excitement comes from the sure knowledge that what they are doing is considered wicked. One story was told of how an eight-year-old girl was discovered in sex play with other children. The girl had gathered from various sources that the aim of the exercise was for the penis to be inserted into the vagina. She had a friend, a boy of similar age, whom she was convinced she would marry when she grew up. She had also learnt that the sex act was something which all married people carried out, and became quite worried that if it were not possible for her and her boyfriend to do this then they would be unable ever to marry. Eventually she persuaded the boy to give it a try. They began to play with one another's genitals wondering exactly how it were possible. Another girl was present and the three discussed among themselves what technique might be involved. All three children were obtaining a kind of excited pleasure from their experiments, but nevertheless genuinely wanted to discover whether or not this thing they had heard was in fact credible. After a while they worked out that the only way was for the boy to lie on top of the girl. It was then that they were discovered by the eight-year-old girl's father. He didn't speak except to tell the girl to go into the house. That night nothing was mentioned about the incident. The girl couldn't understand the silence. She was frightened and guilty, but her father's mute approach prevented her from broaching the matter. She lay awake all night wondering what might become of her. Terrifying fantasies of being sent away forever took over. She was a sensitive child with a powerful imagination, and by morning had reduced herself to a mass of raw nerves. Her mother came into the bedroom: 'Your father told me what you were doing', she said. Her tone was one of accusing calm. 'I hope you will never do anything like that again. I haven't told your headmistress and I won't tell your aunties and uncles . . . not this time'. The incident was never mentioned again, and for that matter sex was never mentioned again. The child went on suffering agonies of guilt: 'I thought that if anyone else ever found out about it they would think me such a dreadful person that they wouldn't even be able to bring themselves to speak to me'. When the girl reached thirteen she went through a period of promiscuity. When her parents found out they assumed the same heavy silence as described previously. At no time did they talk to their daughter about her sexual experiences and feeling – 'We thought that by now you would know what was right and what was wrong!' – was all they had to say. But how their daughter might have made this discovery, when they themselves could not help her, is something which scarcely occurred to them.

This girl's parents were not the only ones who discovered their daughter satisfying her inquisitiveness. 'I suppose I must have been about three years old when I became aware of the fact that boys and girls were very much different. The little boy who lived next door and I were discovered by my mother wandering around without pants on and inspecting each other. She was terribly angry and gave me a good hiding'. A similar occasion arose later in the life of a twenty-one-year-old housewife: 'I discovered the difference between boys and girls when I was about six. A group of playmates, myself included, proceeded to remove our knickers and trousers just to see if this difference we had heard about actually existed. My mother discovered us and told us that what we were doing was disgusting and if the policeman over the road knew what we had been doing he would take us to jail'.

School is the place where most young people gain their 'sex education', but unfortunately the setting is usually the playground rather than the classroom. Today's move towards sex education lectures and classes should be considered remarkable only in that they are so blatantly belated and all too often inadequate. A child's sex education should begin even before she is taught to read, for it is evident that misconceptions are made and fixed in the mind of the child well before she reaches puberty. Only one woman taking part in our study had ever received any kind of official sex education. Even those in the youngest age bracket of nineteen, had been taught no more than the rudimentary facts concerning the reproductive system of a rabbit, necessary for biology 'O' level. Jill, who did receive some sex education at school found it unsatisfactory: 'At junior school we were lucky in hàving a good teacher who told us the basic facts about sex when we were eleven years old. She told us how a baby was made and all about the different bodily functions of girls and boys. We had to write about it in our own words and draw pictures. However, I can't remember anything being said about love!'

Recollections of the attitudes of teachers brought to mind admonishments and warnings against sexual misbehaviour. Teachers were all too willing to tell their pupils what not to do: 'I remember once that I masturbated at school when I was about four years old. My teacher said: "Don't do that or I shall smack you hard". It made me feel rather guilty and I didn't do it again. Of course, at that age, I didn't realise that what I had done had anything to do with sex'. Another woman who attended a convent school told of how all the girls were warned against looking in the bathroom mirror when bathing as it might give them 'carnal desires'. 'We didn't have any sex education at school', said the aforementioned Yorkshire girl, 'but just before we left the Vicar's wife came and told us about love and how marvellous it should be. I was sixteen and didn't realise that a man had to have an ejaculation before the woman could become pregnant. This was the reason for my becoming pregnant when I was seventeen!'

Left in ignorance by teachers and parents these girls were forced to turn to one another and pool their jumbled information, picked up from elder brothers and sisters, television and overheard discussions. Dirty jokes were especially liable to come from slightly older children. Before being interviewed twenty-one-year-old Margaret had spent an evening trying to resurrect buried memories but what kept coming back to her were the smutty stories and one particular school-time experience: 'I learnt about sex through the dirty jokes which were passed around at school. Just after I began secondary school I became friendly with two older girls. Twice they forcibly stripped me, but I can't recall them touching my genitals. I was furious and fought like a tiger, which was unusual as I am not an aggressive type. This experience seems to have had an effect on me as I now like my husband to strip me and force himself upon me'. A girl a year younger than Margaret told me: 'My initiation into sex was when a boy a few years older asked me if I knew what "spunk" was. I pretended to know because I didn't want him to think me ignorant. Of course, I hadn't the faintest idea what he was talking about, although I had this exciting feeling that it was all rather dark and forbidden territory. He then proceeded to tell me a dirty joke about a honeymoon couple. I must have heard hundreds of jokes since and I can rarely remember any of them, but to this day I can remember that particular joke and it still seems horribly distasteful'.

Little girls all eventually become aware that they are, or at least are destined to be, sexual objects — that others apart from themselves are interested in their bodies. This can be quite a revelation for the child who, within the small world of the family, has been made to feel that her own pride and fascination in her body is 'abnormal'. She begins to enjoy the company of both boys and girls who share this fascination and is quick to realise that boys are more interested in her physical make-up than are her female contemporaries. She may, in fact, view other girls as competition in the attention stakes, and it is quite usual that if this occurs at a particularly early age, she will find it difficult to form lasting friendships with members of her own sex later in life. It will be said of her, 'she's not a woman's woman'. It depends very much on the make-up of a child as to the age at which she is made aware that others will take a sexual interest in her. Most of the literature which is available to her as soon as she can read will contain stories which illustrate this. The knight is always after the fair lady; the prince is always after the princess. Most children are able to view adult television and a few samples of typical serials, particularly the American variety, will confirm any idea she may already have formed about men's treatment of women as sexual objects.

Repeatedly in the interviews women would remember how as children they enjoyed kissing boys: 'I remember that at a very early age I wanted boys to kiss me and pay me attention. I gained increasing enjoyment from the company of boys', and 'I always wanted to play kissing games'. Others found the discovery more disturbing. Said one woman, much influenced by her mother: 'When I started menstruating I told my mother and she said, "this is how you use a sanitary towel and don't go with boys" '. Her twelve-year-old daughter took her at her word: 'I wasn't quite sure what she meant by "don't go with boys". I suppose I took it to mean just what it says and didn't speak to a boy for three months'. It was brought home more violently to another: 'We lived in a rough area. One day, while out walking, two boys came up to me and touched me where they shouldn't. I could have killed them. I knew that they were trying to do something, shall we say, dirty. I think that I was about eleven when this happened and the episode upset me a great deal. I didn't tell anyone about it until recently when I told my husband'.

Some obviously took great delight in their new-found sex appeal, as in the case of one girl who, at the age of eight, used to stand naked at her bedroom window, fully aware that the boy in the opposite house was looking out for her. And the girl who made the following remark: 'During childhood I used to obtain a peculiar sexual feeling from watching other children being punished with a leather strap on their hands. At the age of eleven I got the same sort of pleasure when three or four of us girls would go to the toilets at school and show ourselves off to one another. I looked at the others with interest, but got particular pleasure from showing myself off. During one interview I was told that the subject became aware of her sexual role as soon as she knew about sex and immediately wanted to try intercourse: 'I felt more and more aware of my own sexuality, until at the age of twelve I felt that I just had to experiment with sex!'

There were those who first became aware of their sexuality through incestuous experiences, although none of the women interviewed had had intercourse with fathers, brothers or elder male relatives. The following is an extract from an interview with Jessie, a receptionist who was thirty-nine and married. She had an unhappy childhood, mainly because of her father's heavy drinking: 'I first became aware of my own sexuality when I was about fourteen. My father would come into my bedroom at night and want me to make love. I was, of course, frightened. I didn't know anything about sex. However, it did awaken my sexual desires. My father would come into my bedroom and kiss me and say: "I'll show you how lovers kiss". He would put his erect penis in my hand. This happened about three or four times. In the morning my mother would start a row and say that she knew what I had been doing with my father. But I hadn't really done anything. It was terrible . . . being woken in the middle of the night like that. I couldn't really scream or anything. I just tried to cope the best way I could. I thought that my father was a bit of a fool. I felt rather sorry for him. Eventually my father said: "Oh, you're just like your mother", and lost interest. Now that I'm older I can understand why the poor man was so desperate. My mother wasn't interested in sex. I have never in my life worried about sex and this is odd because I can remember as a very young child when I slept in my mother's room, my mother and father fighting like mad because he wanted sex and she didn't. One might think that would have put me off sex but it didn't'.

Jane, a thirty-three-year-old housewife with a less turbulent middle-class background spoke of her relationship with her father: 'I was passionately fond of my father, he died five years ago and I haven't yet recovered from his death. Throughout my childhood I have memories of being close to him; he would get into bed with me until I was twelve or thirteen years old, cuddle me and read to me. In retrospect, there is no doubt that his feelings for me were rather incestuous; I can distinctly remember one incident when he was getting undressed to get into bed with me and my aunt came into the room and screamed because his penis was exposed. It could easily have happened many times before but I can recall that particular time because of the look of horror on my aunt's face. I slept in my parent's room until I was four years old because I had terrible nightmares and couldn't bear to be separated from my father. I used to call for him throughout the night for drinks of water, to be tucked in — anything for his attention. The only things that shut me up was when he would get angry and beat my bottom with a leather strap he had hanging in the room for that express purpose. This was quite a regular ritual and I would receive a real beating, which I am sure I must have enjoyed in some strange way, and yet, as an adult, neither sadism nor masochism has appealed to me'.

Children spend a great deal of their time in a fantasy world, a strange and wonderful world they construct from the facts they have discovered in the world of reality. Thus, as soon as the little girl obtains the knowledge that males desire females and that males will also protect females from danger, they begin to incorporate this information into their fantasies. Once again the influence of legends, books and television is obvious: 'I always indulged in fantasies about television heroes', recalled a twenty-year-old. 'Mainly they were cowboys. I can remember light evenings when I used to lie awake having all kinds of fantasies about being rescued by cowboys on galloping horses. They would tell me I was pretty and act in the same wholesome manner that heroes always act towards their ladies. There was never any sexual acts involved except for kissing. I must have been extremely young when I began having these fantasies, because I can remember being in a pink cot at the time and after the age of three or four I always slept in a bed'.

Another twenty-year-old, presumably exposed to the same heroes, said: 'I have vague childhood memories of sexual curiosity, but I think that this was centred more around the anus than the vagina. At the age of eight I fell in love with both the boy next door and Hopalong Cassidy. I threw sweets out of the bedroom window to the former and lulled myself to sleep at night with fantasies of the latter rescuing me from Red Indians. My earliest concept of love was that it was something which caused one physical pain and which one accepted quite willingly. I remember that I used to arrange my dolls and teddy bears in my bed so that I was forced to lie on as many uncomfortable lumps as possible. I would go to sleep dreaming of scenes of offering myself to be killed or tortured in place of the boy next door or my cowboy hero, who would love me in return for the sacrifice I was making on their behalf. I have never been able to decide whether or not this was caused by an instinctual realisation of eventual loss of virginity or through witnessing my mother repeatedly reduced to tears by my father'.

A further example of mass-media star adoration was provided in an interview with a young housewife: 'Before I was in my teens I used to indulge in daydreams by the hour about romantic encounters with my favourite film star. I wasn't then quite sure what we would do together but my thoughts would so excite me I would shut myself away and masturbate, although I didn't then have an orgasm. In fact, although I masturbated about four or five times a week I didn't have an orgasm until I was about seventeen'.

In a later chapter we will examine more fully the subject of masturbation and the role of fantasy, but it is interesting to note here that masturbation is accompanied by fantasy and that the girl became sexually excited by the idea of being treated as a sexual object by her favourite film star.

In the light of much of the information offered by women and girls interviewed during the course of the survey, one must conclude that because for the most part people are reluctant to acknowledge their own sexual inhibitions (accuse someone of being inhibited and watch their reaction), there is a failure to recognise the amount of damage created by the instilment of inhibitions in childhood and early adolescence. As a parent, will *you* make that mistake?

2 The Morality Maze

We have seen that the women taking part in this study reached puberty almost without exception with little or no understanding of the nature of sexuality. Yet, as adolescents, they were expected to undertake the responsibility of choice between 'right and wrong', 'moral and immoral' and of behaving accordingly. Chris is a typical case. She is now twenty and alienated from her parents. At the age of eighteen she became pregnant. Her parents sent her away to have the baby, which was subsequently adopted. Since then she has wandered the country and is now living with a man in Manchester. In the course of her interview she said: 'My mother bought me powder and lipstick for a schoolfriend's birthday party, yet she sent me to bed as a punishment when she discovered that I had been kissing and indulging in mild sex play with a boy three years older than myself . . . I was about twelve.

'When I was thirteen she noticed a love bite on my neck, which she referred to as a "disgusting suction mark". She refused to speak to me for the rest of the day when I told her that it didn't necessarily mean that I had slept with somebody. Thus, I was torn between enjoyment of the sensations which my body could give and receive, and the wish that I could be malformed and underdeveloped so as not to be forced to distinguish between what I felt to be natural and right, yet was told was wicked and wrong. This conflict eventually led to the feeling that my body was clumsy and inadequate, a complex which lasted until I was sixteen'.

However, despite the strong influences working in favour of retaining virginity until marriage, pre-marital sex was the rule rather than the exception among all age groups interviewed. Subjects found it difficult to point to any reason as to why they acted against upbringing and prevailing social attitudes. Some stated that they gave up their virginity because they were, or thought themselves to be, in love with the man concerned. Others said it was because their friends had lost their virginity, but the majority could only be vague as to their reasons, shrug their shoulders and say: 'It just happened'. Although there were exceptions; one was a girl of twenty who approached the matter clinically and, with a deal of forethought, explained: 'I made up my mind that I was going to lose my virginity to a stranger. I had heard so many stories about how girls always fell in love with the first man they had sex with and I wanted to prove myself different. I didn't want to go through the messy business of losing my virginity with someone whom I liked an awful lot.

'The opportunity arose when I had run away from home because of various conflicts with my parents. I was staying in a coffee bar with an older girl. We slept in the same room and I could hear her making love. I am sure that she must have been a nymphomaniac because she had a different man every night. It didn't excite me but it made me curious. I began to connect sex with the idea of growing up. One night a friend of one of the older girls' boyfriends came into the coffee bar and asked me if I minded if he stayed overnight. I found him quite attractive so I let him make love to me. It was all rather miserable because while I was in bed with him the other girl was having a row with her boyfriend. I wasn't at all sexually excited and lay completely passive. I thought that the whole thing was rather sordid, but I wasn't expecting very much so I wasn't particularly disappointed. It hurt and I bled . . . it was pretty much the way I expected it to be. In a way I regarded virginity as an incumberance. There were some girls at school who were extremely promiscuous and in a way I admired them. I didn't like the fact that they would sleep with absolutely anyone, but I envied their freedom and their "don't give a damn" attitude. I have never really thought of the way in which I lost my virginity as having anything much to do with my sex-life. I adopted a purely clinical attitude towards it. It was an obstacle which had to be overcome'.

The other exception was a former Cambridge undergraduate who was twenty-one and first had sex at seventeen: 'I came to the conclusion that sex was too important a thing to be taken lightly; I had no wish to lose my virginity at a drunken party in the way some girls are reputed to do. So, I set about finding an older man who was well experienced in sex and who could teach me the art of love. Luckily, I found such a man and asked him. He agreed with pleasure. I spent the next weekend at his flat and we made love, unrushed and undisturbed by external things. I was surprised that it was over so quickly, with so little fuss. He was gentle with me the first time and took a great deal of trouble to make sure that it didn't hurt me. I only realised how much he had restrained himself later, when his love-making was intense and violent. I didn't find it at all painful, which was probably due to his care and self-restraint. I remember being surprised that there was no blood; I enjoyed it up to a point, but it didn't come up to my expectations. He told me that it is rare for the first time to be completely satisfactory and that it would get better. It did too! This first experience had a strong effect on my subsequent sex life. I am sure the way this man made love to me made a great difference to what I came to expect of men. Any man I slept with afterwards I compared to the first one, and I find it sad to say that almost the only real pleasure I have had from a man other than my first lover, has come from my husband. No one else has been interested in what I was feeling'.

The reason that so few actually made up their minds to rid themselves of their virginity probably was because the issue appeared so confusing. The conflict between what had been instilled into the minds of most girls and what they felt as a natural urge led them to dismiss all possibility of clear thinking on the matter. The tendency was to drift into intercourse along a path of gradually intensified sexual experiences. Almost all the women allowed certain liberties such as caressing of their breasts and masturbation for quite some time before they progressed to full inter-course. There is little doubt that many girls would not have indulged in intercourse when they did if it had not been for the activities of their friends and acquaintances. 'I allowed it to happen', said one girl, 'because all my friends were doing it and because they talked so much about it. It was for the same reason that I started smoking. I thought something was happening to other people which I was missing. Prior to having inter-course I had carried out mutual masturbation with several boys so I suppose it was a natural progression'.

Susan who was nineteen spoke of how naive she discovered herself to be when she came to work in London and shared a flat with three other girls: 'They talked a lot about sex. They were all sleeping with their boyfriends. I met a boy who after two months asked me out. The first night that we went out we had sex. I think that I allowed him to make love to me purely out of curiosity. I had heard the other girls talk so much about sex that I thought I had better find out about it myself'.

Among young adolescent girls those who have lost their virginity become almost as a secret sect. Their virgin friends react jealously to the esoteric whisperings. They also want to become initiates and gladly suffer a broken hymen in order to join the group. Twenty-nine-year-old May's feelings were: 'It was very much a case of keeping up with the Joneses. All my other friends were having mad passionate affairs and I thought to myself, "Well, at your age it's about time you started" '.

Ocassionally initial sexual experiences are a direct result of innocence. Liza was ten when her mother died and she was brought up by her elder brother: 'It turned out that my brother was attracted to me and tried to seduce me when I was twelve. Once he came into my room as I was making my bed. I was wearing a sheer nightdress and he yelled at me for wearing a nightdress like that. Then one morning during a school holiday, I was sleeping late and he came into my room. It wasn't uncommon for him to come into my room and play with me, but this time he got into bed and I felt that there was something different about it. He said "let's play" and we did sort of acrobatics and balancing things. He then said "let's pull down your pyjama pants", which he quickly did and I quickly pulled them back up again. There followed a big tussle in bed and then he snuggled up to me from behind. I knew what was going on and didn't want it to happen so I got out of bed, whereupon he left the room. He returned later, apologised and asked me not to tell anyone. The incident was closed. We never ever talked about it again. I don't feel that it did me any damage. I think that even at the time I understood that he was frustrated, although I wasn't fully aware of how intense the sex drives of young men would be'.

Joyce was so incredibly ignorant and innocent that it was inevitable she should suffer. Her mother had always forbidden her to have any contact with boys and she discovered sex in her teens through a friend who used to sneak looks at the books handled by her bookbinder father. Joyce was seventeen when the following incident took place: 'I was in the park when a man came and sat next to me. He started talking about the weather and similar topics and I answered him. After a while I got up and said that I was going home. He offered to walk part of the way with me and before I knew where I was I found myself on the ground with him on top of me. He broke my hymen and that was that. I didn't know anything about rape and the law, in fact I didn't know anything about men. All I knew was that if my mother found out she would raise the roof, so I didn't tell her. It was over and done with so quickly but I was scared out of my wits by the pain'.

In England it is illegal for a man to have sexual intercourse with any girl under the age of sixteen. To do so risks imprisonment for the man and a juvenile court appearance, perhaps resulting in probation, for the girl. Yet, time and again there were instances of girls whose first experience of intercourse was well before this age. A thirty-nine-year-old woman said: 'When I was fourteen, I belonged to a tennis club and there were lots of boys there who were always fooling around with the girls. It was sex all round. Eventually, I had intercourse. Now that I'm older it all seems slightly sordid. It happened round the back of a rose bush or something. I enjoyed it. It wasn't at all painful. I was never frightened of becoming pregnant because the boys had worked out the technique of coitus interruptus'.

A twenty-year-old, who also first had intercourse at the age of fourteen, found it less enjoyable: 'I was very frightened and found it painful. I was really quite disgusted and felt that I was justified in making the analogy that it was like dogs I had seen on the street. I did not love the boy nor even feel affection for him. He was a lot older than me and I found this inflated my ego; therefore, in a way, I became a little bit infatuated. I suppose I was flattered by his attentions'.

Another who lost her virginity at the same age as the two previous girls commented: 'The boy whom I first had intercourse with was also fourteen. We used to get involved in heavy petting and I would get terribly aroused, so one day we had intercourse. I was upset about it afterwards and felt very guilty about having lost my virginity. I had been brought up strictly and with a strong religious influence. It seemed to me that I had done a bad thing. My parents had never actually told me that sex was wrong, but I picked up the idea from books and general Biblical study, consequently I felt that I was wicked. I can't really say that at that time I enjoyed sex; I got no particular feeling from it. Yet, in spite of this and despite my guilt, I carried on having sex with this boy for three months. Although it eventually became pleasurable, I never completely enjoyed it, I didn't have an orgasm, but I think that I got a kick out of the fact that what I was doing was illicit'.

A young girl, aware of her attractive body but without any conception of the nature of the sex drive of the opposite sex, is probably the most vulnerable creature in the world. She exploits her new-found ability to attract the attention of men and is preoccupied with the power of her own body. At the same time she is frightened of her own desire. Sex becomes a kind of roller-coaster ride. There is the sensual pleasure of petting and of having the genitals tentatively explored, there is the ego-boosting achievement of reducing a member of the opposite sex to a state of panting and, most important, the excitement of seeing just how far she can push these two factors.

Sylvia related how, at the age of sixteen after the break-up of her parent's marriage and release from her father's strict influence she decided really to 'go to town'. 'I took a junior job in an office where I was easy prey for all the men. I was very pretty and, I suppose, vain. I was flattered by their attentions. I flirted with at least four of the men and got myself felt and fooled around with in unused offices and cupboards during working hours. During the lunch hours I used to walk down Oxford Street and get myself picked up. One time I met a man about fifteen years older than myself who was an actor. I was attracted to him right away and talked to him of my secret longing to be an actress. He said he'd get me started and that we should have dinner together that evening. Dinner was at his flat, where he filled me with drink and forcibly raped me. It hurt and I was frightened, especially as he nearly strangled me to stop me from screaming, and my clothes seemed to be covered in blood. He must have felt very sorry for when it was all over, he helped me to wash my pants and slip and dry them before I could go home'.

Just as the naive virgin will equate attention from the opposite sex with self-assertion so the girl, who has taken the plunge and lost her virginity, will often view intercourse itself as an exercise in one-upmanship which is often the underlying reason behind overt promiscuity. This is illustrated in the continuation of Sylvia's story: 'I suppose I could be considered to have been a promiscuous teenager because I cannot remember how many men and boys I had affairs with during those early years. Neither can I remember any really deep feeling connected with sex; I wanted the company of men all the time, evenings out, parties and I loved all the attention. They wanted sex from me and it was, most of the time, something I gave them because it seemed to give me a sort of control over them, made me feel important. Perhaps I needed sex to give me an identity, an individuality'.

Promiscuity is such a vague word that the problem of definition should be confronted. When does a woman become promiscuous – after three men or thirty? Where does one draw the line? It is impossible to say. I mentioned earlier, generalisations can be dangerous particularly when considering sexual behaviour. Should a woman, whose need for sex is great, be morally judged as promiscuous because she has not yet met a man with whom she felt she could remain and so fill that need when desire and opportunity arise? I think not. Perhaps the most useful definition depends on the self-judgement of the person in question: when a woman referred to herself as promiscuous or insinuated that she considered herself to have been promiscuous then this was so. For promiscuity was always the word used when the woman felt that she had broken her own standards, when she had been untrue to herself.

An extremely intelligent divorcee of thirty-eight had this to say on the subject: 'I have always slept around. I don't like the word promiscuous because it has all sorts of bad connotations. The simple truth is that I like to make love. I like to find out about people and it is only after one has made love with a person that one can really get that person to talk about themselves. I think that I have probably helped a lot of people in this way. I'm not so concerned with what I get out of it. I tend to be rather altruistic about the whole thing'.

In cases where women considered themselves to have been promiscuous there were almost always associations of guilt, and horror at what might have resulted: 'I was so promiscuous, at the age of fourteen' said one girl, 'that it frightens me to think about what the consequences could have been. It really was quite tragic because I didn't know what the hell I was doing — except that I wasn't supposed to be doing it'.

Occasionally intercourse at such an early age is the result of games which the participants did not intend to go so far: 'I was eleven when I had sexual intercourse for the first time, which sounds awfully young, but it wasn't really of my own choosing. My girlfriends held me down while this fellow, who was about twenty-five, had intercourse with me. We knew him vaguely and he often used to came into the barn where we played to fool around with us. This time we were in the barn having a laugh and I think that he got a bit excited. I was terrified, but then I found that it didn't hurt, probably because penetration was at minimum. Afterwards I didn't really feel anything. I think that all my friends were promiscuous and this was their way of initiating me'.

Girls strongly aware of their sexuality at an early age are often easily persuaded to experiment with men many years their senior. This happened to Hilary: 'As far as I can remember as soon as I was told about sex, I became aware of my sexual role and wanted to try intercourse. My first experience of sex was when I was twelve. My father had a friend who used to come around to the house a lot. He began by gradually making remarks to me about sex whenever there was no one else around. One day he came round when my parents were out. He started talking about sex and said at the age of thirteen I should be starting to think about trying it.

I was curious about it so I took him through to my bedroom where we undressed and got into bed. We had intercourse after a great deal of sex play. I felt very matter-of-fact about it. It didn't impress me at all. It only hurt slightly. I didn't really have a relationship with this man apart from his being a friend of my father's. After all, I was a twelve-year-old schoolgirl and he was a married man of forty, with two daughters older than myself'.

It is evident from these interviews that many young girls develop strong sexual desires soon after puberty, and that these desires are sufficiently forceful to drive a girl beyond the restrictions of law, fear of parental discovery and social taboos. It is therefore an anomaly that may mean a court case and that the girl be made to feel criminal. Improved living standards mean that physical maturity is now reached at a far earlier age than ever before. A trend towards greater freedom for teenagers also brings about a feeling of independance and the ability to make decisions alone. But usually a blind eye is turned to the sexual activities of schoolgirls with the notable exception of the occasional sensationalised stories in Sunday newspapers.

The interviews also reveal that contraceptive methods, other than coitus interruptus, are rarely employed during these initial experiences. These girls are in danger and nothing but an outmoded and cruel law exists to protect them. Their ignorance leaves them exposed to the risk of contracting venereal diseases and becoming pregnant; in consequence of social mores they are forced into furtive encounters in dark doorways, back seats of cars and anywhere else they can find to hide away. I am *not* suggesting that girls of fourteen should be encouraged to participate in indescriminate sexual relationships, but I am suggesting that it is the responsibility of teachers, parents, legislators and society in general to wake up to the fact that intercourse under the age of sixteen, with the full consent of the girl, takes place frequently and that incidence will continue to increase. Thus it is necessary to ensure that some of the dangers are alleviated through both the availability of contraception and sound sex education.

However, despite their own inexperience and the often clumsy approach of their lovers, none of these women found their initial sexual experience so terrifying as to prevent them from carrying on the relationship or going on almost immediately to another. Disappointments were almost always accepted philosophically. It was only physical pain which caused any trepidation as far as further experimentations were concerned, as in the case of Wendy, a forty-six-year-old housewife and former actress:

'When I first had sex at the age of seventeen I was both afraid and curious. I didn't even know the physical facts of virginity and was worried to death when afterwards I experienced pain and bleeding. I had no idea that it would hurt and when it did I thought that it would be like that every time. Consequently, I was bitterly disappointed and, of course, didn't experience orgasm although beforehand I became very excited. He was a handsome dashing young Naval officer and I was swept off my feet. He went away and was later killed. I didn't have intercourse for two years and then it took some persuading. However, I was delighted to find that this time it didn't hurt and from then on I never looked back'.

One woman spoke of the fact that all her school friends had warned her that the first time was 'a bit of a trial', so she didn't expect much else. Most women looked quite surprised when asked if they had had an orgasm the first time they had intercourse. They couldn't believe that anyone should think that they might have had. In fact, the majority stated that at the time they first had intercourse they weren't aware that women experienced orgasm during intercourse: 'I was rather disappointed in the whole thing', said May, whose initiation occurred when she was eighteen. 'It was due to my inexperience rather than his. It didn't hurt because I had had various operations and was used to being pulled about down there. I didn't have orgasm. I didn't know that I was supposed to. I didn't find out about orgasm until I had one toward the end of this first relationship. I began to realise then what I had missed'.

The girl previously quoted as considering her virginity 'an incumberance', although perhaps a little more extreme and blunt than most, was not far from typical, at least in attitude; for many it was the fact that they had gone through intercourse, good or bad, which was most important to them. Above all, they felt different: 'it was the fact of eventually having done this thing which had loomed so large for so long', remarked one.

Some could remember the event in extraordinary detail. 'I was sixteen when I lost my virginity. I was home from school for the Easter holiday and met a boy whom I knew only by sight. We had coffee together and talked. He was a member of the Campaign for Nuclear Disarmament which I wanted to join. He took me to his flat to show me some literature from C.N.D., and, with the music of Bob Dylan pouring from the record-player he attempted to make love to me. When I told him that I was a virgin he didn't attempt to persuade or force me, but simply asked if I wanted him to go on. I couldn't think of any reason why he shouldn't. All my previous thinking seemed invalid under the circumstances.

'He didn't indulge in any preparatory love play, he just pushed up my skirt, pulled down my pants and got on top of me. I felt awkward and inexperienced. I was completely unaroused and lay still. I felt a sharp pain and then it was over. I certainly didn't have an orgasm. I felt sore and ached and noticed that I was bleeding. This turned out to be the start of a menstrual period which had probably been brought on by the emotional shock. I didn't have any idea how one was supposed to act after intercourse, so I followed his example and lit a cigarette. My first act on leaving him was to telephone my friend to tell her the news. Neither did I feel too let down because I had heard from friends that the first time is never the best. I was glad that I had lost my virginity'.

Mary made the common rationalisation that she was in love so that her first experience did not have to appear as insignificant as it really was: 'Looking back and being truthful I don't think that I loved the boy. I think that I tried to tell myself that I loved him. I was seventeen and terribly curious about sex, and I knew that he wanted me. I felt guilty afterwards and I kept wondering if I was going to give away the fact that he and I had made love. The first time I didn't enjoy it. It was painful and I didn't have an orgasm. At the time I didn't know what an orgasm was. This boy taught me very little about sex; he was really quite immature; whenever we had sex it was always illicit and clandestine. The thought that she may be caught having illicit sex is one of the biggest deterrents against a woman having an orgasm although, of course, there is also the fear of pregnancy.'

Those women genuinely in love with their first sexual partner were less clinical and less cynical about their initiation. One might safely surmise that in numerous instances where the girl was emotionally involved with the boy, then the boy would also be emotionally involved with her, which would lead him to treat her more gently. Also in such cases the shock of extreme sexual excitment was tempered by a more romantic atmosphere. Even in cases where feelings were not reciprocated to the same degree, greater relaxation and pleasure was achieved due to the woman feeling that she was giving something of herself to a person she loved: 'My first experience of intercourse was when I was twenty-one', said Hazel, now twenty-nine and happily married. It was terribly painful but all the same I made him finish. I didn't expect to enjoy it the first time. I wasn't afraid, in fact I was very excited. I was happy to give so much pleasure to someone of whom I was fond. I felt elated for days afterwards. He was a fellow student and we had been going out together for about nine months and petting heavily. We had indulged in mutual masturbation and once he forced me to take his penis into my mouth because I wouldn't have it any other way. I thought I was going to choke. But he was kind and gentle afterwards. The occasion when we first had sex took place after we had had a slight accident on his motor bike. I was upset. He comforted me and then we lay down in this lovely hazel wood full of blue bells and made love'.

For the woman in love the setting for her first experience can be of paramount importance. Twenty-one-year-old Nina felt that a relaxing environment contributed much to the success of hers: 'I was seventeen and I suppose you could say that it was all planned. I knew that I was going to sleep with this fellow and so we both arranged it. We took advantage of a flat left empty by a friend who was away at the time. The surroundings were pleasant. The flat was warm, the bed comfortable, we had good music, good food — in fact everything we wanted. 'My reaction was one of amazement. I felt that I had stumbled across something I could never comprehend. It intrigued me. It was altogether bewildering. Having no yardstick at the time I could not measure my pleasure, but looking back it still appears as a wonderful experience, not in terms of orgasm or excitement, but in the joy of the unknown. It wasn't very painful, only a little at first. The boy meant a great deal to me. At the time I thought that I loved him as much as I could possibly love anybody. But now he is my husband and I love him very much more. I suppose that this first experience did have an effect on my subsequent sex-life insomuch as it made me intensely curious. I entered a great pleasure-seeking phase and developed quite an appetite. My husband tells me that this is exactly what he intended. He gave me a great deal of pleasure and taught me everything. Perhaps the reason that he was so good to me was because he was so much more experienced'.

Gwen was also seventeen when she first had sex. She too loved her partner and later became his wife, but with rather less happy results than Nina, as we will see in a later chapter: 'I had known him for three months. We were in his room sitting on the bed cuddling and it just happened. It was his first experience too and the whole thing was spontaneous. We both responded remarkably without really knowing what was happening. It wasn't intellectual at all, but a totally emotional experience and very beautiful. I suppose that there was some pain, but I didn't really take very much notice. I had a complete orgasm and felt marvellous'.

There is no doubt that the element of love frequently averted disaster, especially in instances where all the odds suggested that the girl's future sexual happiness was in danger. Many overcame repugnance, guilt and fear through love. 'I was always frightened of sex,' said one girl. 'My parents had made me fear anything to do with sexual contact, yet I was willing to allow my fiancé to do as he wished because I trusted him to such a great extent'.

Rita, a thirty-three-year-old housewife, told of how she came to regard sex with disgust: 'When I was quite young, my mother took me to the pictures where she met a soldier. It was during the war and my father had deserted us some years previously. The soldier, my mother and myself slept in the same bed. During the night I awoke and realised that my mother and the soldier were having intercourse. I was disgusted that they should do this when I was in bed with them. I had the same feeling on another occasion when I was eighteen. My mother, step-father, step-brother and myself were all on holiday and sleeping in the same room. My mother and step-father began to have intercourse. I could hear them talking about it and urging one another on'.

It was only through falling in love and trusting her fiancé implicitly that Rita overcame these disturbing incidents: 'My own first experience of intercourse was when I was twenty-one. My present husband and I were courting and gradually we advanced from passionate kissing to mutual caressing until we reached the stage of fondling one another's genitals. This usually took place in dark alleys or ruined buildings as we had nowhere else to go. We had our regular haunt, a market place where we used to hide among stacks of crates. However, despite the furtive surroundings and my previous disgust over sex, I never felt guilty or ashamed. I think that my passions had been so late in awakening that when they were at last aroused I was completely carried away. From fondling one another's sex organs it was a short step to attempting intercourse. It wasn't very successful, probably due to the awkwardness of our situation. After several unsuccessful attempts we ceased to try and my future husband would content himself with caressing my vagina with his penis. I achieved orgasm on several occasions through that method.

'After carrying on like this for some time, we decided to go away for the weekend. Although we didn't actually admit to one another that the main reason for going was sexual fulfilment, this was uppermost in our minds. We managed to obtain a double room quite easily and went to bed fairly early, both eager for sex. We did not need much foreplay to arouse us to full passion. After several attempts, my fiancé managed to enter me. We were both surprised at the ease of penetration and decided that previous attempts must have broken my hymen. Although I didn't have an orgasm, I obtained great pleasure from the intercourse and soon fell into a very contented sleep. In the morning when we awoke we had intercourse again and I felt very happy afterwards even though, once again, I didn't have an orgasm. On neither occasion was there any pain and at no time did I feel any apprehension as to what might happen. I feel this is because we worked together towards this event over a long period and we had got to know one another's bodies well'.

In retrospect the interviewees tended to regard youthful promiscuity as a period of muddled uncertainty, although on occasions, as in Sylvia's case, the girl would deliberately set out to be picked up. Joyce, a forty-four-year-old divorcee, already quoted about losing her virginity in an attack, gave the following amazing story of her sexual activities during teens: 'After the attack, I began to realise that my friends were having intercourse with boys — at least they said that they were although I rather suspect that they weren't telling the truth. I wanted to be in fashion, so I too started having sex. I didn't really want the sex. I did it because everyone else was doing it.

'I used to pick up boys in the cinema and on street corners. I was really no better than a prostitute. I didn't know what I was doing. It was during the war and there were a number of American and British soldiers in the town where I lived so it was quite easy. I would just stand in the street and stare at the men as they passed by and give them the 'come on'. Once I picked up a man we would probably have a cup of coffee and chat before finding a secluded spot where we would have sex. These men never wanted to see me again, which was something that I could never really understand. I didn't find any part of it exciting; I suppose that it was an act of rebellion against my upbringing. It came to an end when I read in the local paper that there was to be an effort to clean up the streets. After that there was only the cinema in which to operate. I kept on without ever getting any pleasure out of sex simply because I didn't think that a woman was supposed to obtain pleasure in love-making'.

Whether or not women experienced adolescent 'promiscuity' often depended upon the strength of their sex drive.

Sonia, former Cambridge undergraduate, described her intense need for regular sex: 'During my early teens I had a deep need for physical contact with the opposite sex, which wasn't fulfilled until I was seventeen. Being aware of this need, I spent the early years of adolescence in a state of frustration and longing. Coupled with this frustration was the fact that I was ugly and therefore not popular with boys of my own age who wanted a pretty face to show off to their friends. I think I would have been happier without my knowledge of sex and my need for it, but then such happiness would have been a fool's paradise. I have had sexual

25

relations with twenty-seven men since the first one. Some of these relationships were important to me, others less so. It depended on the quality of the relationship as a whole, rather than on the sexual aspect alone. Most of my affairs seemed important to me at the time but, on looking back, I can see that few had lasting effects. However, having so many experiences made me more mature, I think, and helped me appreciate people as human beings, rather than just as isolated units acting in vacuums. It made me more aware of the feelings of others. I was looking for a man who could give me the same degree of satisfaction that I had received from my first lover'.

Although there is more likelihood of women having sex with many men during the period before they meet one man with whom they fall in love, such activity is not always confined to the single girl. A sixty-year-old language teacher recalled: 'My husband died seven years after we were married. But even before that we led separate lives. By then the Second World War was on and with the free atmosphere which prevails during war time, I found it easy to be adventurous. It become a sort of symbol to see how many men you could have sex with. I had sex with more men than I care to remember. Sometimes I was satisfied, sometimes not. When a woman is being that promiscuous, and is the least bit sensitive, she becomes rather disgusted with herself because her sex is entirely on a physical level, with no emotional involvement or stability within the relationships. I didn't feel guilty about being unfaithful to my husband. I tended to poke my tongue out at the moralists. If I had felt guilty I wouldn't have been so promiscuous. At the beginning it took me a long time to lose my inhibitions and achieve orgasm. It must be realised that if, in reality, you are not a prostitute or a wild woman you have a certain amount of shyness. It is very difficult to be free with someone you hardly know. However, I found that some affairs of longer duration did emerge and with these men I experienced orgasm'.

For the woman with a broken marriage a free attitude towards sex is often employed as a means of resolving loneliness. I quote the following case in detail because, relevant to this point, it is also poignant and thought-provoking. The interviewee is a twenty-three-year-old office worker. She comes from a working-class home in the West Riding of Yorkshire, and became pregnant at the age of seventeen.

'When I became pregnant it was a great shock to my parents. In Yorkshire where I come from, it matters what the neighbours say. Everyone told me that I should get married for the sake of the child. I didn't know what to do. Eventually, I persuaded my boyfriend to marry me mainly because of my parents. We got married in church when I was four months pregnant. I didn't wear white though; I wore pink. I don't think that my husband resented being married, but it seemed as if his parents were conspiring against me. They lived in a big farm-house and we went to live with them. Their ways weren't the ways I was used to. It was the first time that I had ever been away from home. After we got married we used to read books like the *Kama Sutra* and I feel that such books can really help. Unfortunately, I lost the baby when I was seven months pregnant. I nearly died. It was a case of the baby or me. After that I began to take the Pill. It suited me, but one day I forgot to take it and I became pregnant again. This time I had an abortion.

'Our marriage was really a big mistake. We were always arguing. My husband was violent; he broke my wrist twice. He used to keep me awake all night if he wanted sex, whether I wanted it or not. He didn't know how to treat a woman, because he had never had another woman – only me. Yet, I think that deep down he will always love me. I eventually decided to leave him because I kept losing babies. I lost three altogether. I was terribly depressed and started taking sleeping pills. I tried to commit suicide three times and they kept rushing me to hospital and used stomach pumps to save me. I would say that the real reason for the breakdown of my marriage was sex. I was scared of getting pregnant again. I didn't want to die. My parents kept frightening me. They used to tell my husband: 'If you have any more children our daughter may die'. Every time he asked me for sex I was terrified. I don't think that it made me frigid; after all I can enjoy sex now. My husband was so big that he used to squash me, I prefer lighter men. He never actually accused me of being frigid, but he used to keep me awake all night begging me to have sex with him. I couldn't sleep and I used to go downstairs crying. He would chase after me and make me go back up with him. He forced me to have sex against my will. By the time I left him I was getting no enjoyment out of sex.

'Eventually I came down to London; I had it planned for quite a while. My husband saw me off at the bus stop. When I arrived in London I wanted a job where I could live in and I started work in a hospital. After arriving in London, I became very promiscuous. I think that it was a sort of psychological reaction to what had gone on before. I was living in a hostel with a group of other girls, so I decided to write a reply to some of the adverts that men put in the personal columns of newspapers, asking for female companions. I was lonely and not at all choosey. I used to go out with all kinds of older men, purposely for a good time and sex. I don't know why this was. Between July and March I had sex with about twenty different men. I didn't feel at all guilty. I like going with these men. In a way I enjoyed sex with all of them Some wanted me simply for sex, others wanted a companion. I met an Indian boy who introduced me to a whole new way of life, new clothes, new food, in fact an entirely new culture. He was very ardent. We used to have sex two or three times whenever we spent the night together. It didn't do my health any good. At this time I was on the Pill. I met one man who wanted to beat me. I was really scared of him. I went to live with him for two weeks. He threw me out because I didn't want sex at least three times every night. I have not been able to bring myself to do some of the things that men have wanted me to do; things like feliatio and anal intercourse. I hate violence in bed, I like gentleness. On the other hand I am very mercenary. For instance I sometimes go out with this man who is rich. Well, I am poor and I don't see why I should give in without getting something out of him first. I want the best of both worlds, someone who will provide for me but not ask everything of me.

'As far as I know I have never had an orgasm. If it is this marvellous feeling which comes over you like a wave, which is the way I have heard some girls describe it, then I have certainly never experienced it. I once read a book which described an orgasm and it seemed to me a mightier thing than I have ever experienced. Even if I can't get an orgasm I just like to feel that I am close to someone. I like companionship as well as sex. I stopped sleeping with a lot of men because I thought that I was either going to get pregnant or catch V.D. You see I had to stop taking the Pill because I couldn't get it anywhere as the doctors in London don't know my medical record. I now use pessaries and ask the men to use sheaths. That way it is not so easy to catch V.D. I had a boyfriend who caught V.D. and he made me go to the clinic. However, I was clear. I know that the clinic is specially for V.D. and nobody cares who you are, but I felt sort of dirty.

'The last time that I had sex was two weeks ago; I met the man the same day. I hope that I am not lapsing into my old ways. I think it must have been the booze. Most of the men I have known since I came to London have just come and gone. I would like a permanent friendship with somebody. I get so fed up when I come home from work and I am on my own. I have no one to talk to at home so when I go to work I want to talk, but people don't like that because they think that work is not the place for chats. None of the twenty relationships I had in the past year lasted because I wasn't really attracted to any of the men physically. You can't tell from an advert what a person is going to be like. Perhaps I didn't mind so much in private, but most of them weren't really handsome and so I felt that I didn't want to be seen out with them. I could have made so much money if I had been on the game. I have been asked to go on the game, but I wouldn't want to because then you have to have sex even if you don't feel like it.

'I hope that one day I will get out of the vacuum of loneliness I am in at present. There is really no one to whom I can turn. From what I can see everything depends on money. A person can have love as a side-line but first they must have money. If you've got ten shillings left on Monday to last you until Thursday then there is not much you can do in the way of planning for the future. I shall just go on and hope something will turn up. I have found that the more you chase something the less likely you are to catch it. I shall go on until something turns up'.

I have quoted here two extreme examples, the divorcee who found happiness through many men and this last case where the alternation from man to man emphasised rather than solved the original problem of loneliness. Neither can be judged, but the latter might be thought to have made a mistake as far as her personal fulfilment is concerned. For it is this fulfilment which every woman should seek. If her methods are conventional she should be considered lucky for she escapes the prejudice which falls upon the head of her more unconventional sister, who should be admired for her courage and self-perception.

3 Love and Marriage

Women in love — a vast almost mystic subject, with which troubadours, poets, philosophers, psychologists and every man who has found himself the object of this love have pondered over for centuries. I do not propose here to add to the mass of theoretical writing on the nature of feminine love, for after all however interesting they may be theories are but theories. I intend rather to document the remarks of the women interviewed in this survey, which may confirm or negate the reader's own thoughts on the matter.

Primarily we are concerned here with the role of sexuality in the love relationship. When a woman falls in love does her attitude towards sex change? Is her experience of sex different? What is the importance of sex as an integral part of the relationship? We have already touched upon the subject when in the last chapter we examined cases of women who lost their virginity to the man they loved and we were able to note that this often resulted in greater initial pleasure, through emotional satisfaction. It is also relevant that frequently women who were previously unable to achieve orgasm were able to do so within the context of a love relationship.

Undoubtedly, the age at which a woman first finds herself in love has a major influence on her behaviour. I firmly believe that love can occur at any age. Admittedly, youthful infatuation is likely to become confused with love. Young girls are so often in love with the idea of falling in love. Although some of the greatest literature recognises and treats as such, 'young love', in real life it is relegated to romantic fantasy. Certainly, young love is rash. It is bewildering, and lack of emotional maturity makes it difficult for the girl to cope with the strength of feeling involved.

The following extract is taken from the interview of a twenty-one-year-old secretary, who at the age of fourteen was having sex with numerous boys, mostly older than herself. She then met the boy of whom she speaks and is still in love with him six years later. She describes here the beginnings of her affair: 'It was like a fairy tale. We went for long country walks and talked until our heads were empty. I don't think that I had ever opened up to another human being the way I opened up to him. Neither had I felt so devoted to anyone. The first time that we made love I thought that I was going to die there and then because that was what life was all about. There wasn't much else to touch beyond it. I had never before had an orgasm and, in fact, for a while I went on having orgasms without knowing what they were. As far as I was concerned it was a magical experience induced through the spell of him. In a way I suppose I felt guilty about loving him so much. At that age there is this big parent thing because they expect you to have a career and there is a lot of mass media stuff churned out about young love being very beautiful but totally unreal. I felt that no one understood the way that I loved, not even him. It was a huge and perhaps rather magnificent load to carry around without being able to communicate it to anyone. I felt that if I tried to tell anyone they would laugh and say that no one loved another person as much as that, let alone a fifteen-year-old schoolgirl, who "couldn't possibly know her own mind anyway". I badly wanted to tell my mother. I wanted her to say that she was glad that I could love that intensely. I wanted her to understand more than anyone, but I realised from her attitude that she couldn't. She used to get quite annoyed about us walking up our road hand in hand. I don't think that she was bothered by it from a moral point of view. It was just that she hadn't foreseen something like that happening until I had gone to university and got all the desirable bits of paper'.

No doubt many young girls would have gone on having unsatisfactory experiences of sex if they had not met someone whom they love. We have already heard how the following girl lost her virginity at the age of sixteen during a single meeting with a fellow C.N.D. supporter. Disappointment with this first sexual encounter led her to believe that sex was not the remarkable experience she had been led to expect: 'If I had lost my virginity under the kind of circumstances which I had dreamed of, that is tender and romantic, then I am sure that my ensuing actions would have been different. However, I began to think that such circumstances were adolescent dreams. During the next few months I ran away from home twice and slept with about eight men. Most of these relationships were of the one-night-stand variety. I never experienced an orgasm. For me sex was completely physical, although to some extent I remained discriminating and did not take advantage of every opportunity which arose. It is possible that this "promiscuity" may also have been a reaction against my mother's attitude to my sexual development and an act of defiance against my upbringing and education.

'Two months before my seventeenth birthday, I met Brian. I was attracted to him at once and spent a whole night staying in waiting for him to ring me, which eventually he did. We went to the cinema and when he kissed me my body began to throb. When he touched my nipples I experienced sensations hitherto unknown to me. It was three months before we had complete sexual intercourse. My parents were away for the weekend and we went to a party and got quite drunk. When we returned we went to my bedroom and he undressed me and told me to get into bed. I was sure that my body was beautiful because he found it so. I lay in bed and watched him strip. When he lay beside me I could feel my whole body vibrate towards him. We didn't hurry. The night became an orgasm which recreated and charged itself until finally we slept. When we awoke we made love again.

'Brian and I stayed together for more than a year. During that time we made love as often as possible, at home in front of the fire while my parents were watching television in the next room; in his room when his parents were out; in the park lying on the grass; and once at the late night bus stop. Each time I experienced at least one orgasm. I became aware of the more subtle potentialities of sex and of the beauty of the male genitals. Until then I had always regarded the male genitals as man's means of obtaining gratification through me. Once on the underground in London, when I was fourteen and wearing my school uniform, an old man sitting next to me masturbated into a newspaper. It was only when I was having sex with Brian that I could bring myself to hold and examine an erect penis'.

Love provides a reason for sex, where before there has been no other reason apart from curiosity and the fact that 'everyone else is doing it' or 'boys expect it when they take you out'. Some interviewees spoke of early sexual experience as being without desire. The physical excitement was there and for some that was sufficient, but the more sensitive the girl the less likely she was to be satisfied with physical sensations alone. As with the last two cases Greta lost her virginity during her early teens. She became disillusioned with her parents, sex, society and her own existence. Two years later she met a boy for whom she felt emotional desire: 'The fact that I desired him for his own sake was important to me. I actually wanted to go to bed with him before he made any move towards me. I was overwhelmed by this marvellous sensation because I had never known what it was to desire someone. Eventually we made love. I had never had an orgasm and I didn't experience it this first time with him yet I was satisfied. By this time I was aware of the fact that women did have a climax, but I had no idea what it might be like. The first time that it happened I was shocked because I never thought that one sensation could so take over one's entire being. For the first time I was lost in someone else. I felt as if my mind and my body, which had always seemed completely separate entities, suddenly fused and become as one. Then it was as if this whole abstract thing which was me turned into a sort of liquid, something pure like liquid gold, flowing into this person until he too brimmed over with my love. I adored him and I am sure that this fact strengthened the intensity of the orgasm'.

Love provoked an entirely new experience for these girls, sex became a celebration rather than an act unto itself, and their sensitive accounts show them to have been granted a further maturity, rather than having been struck with what their elders are so fond of calling 'fanciful notions'. Another lucid quotation further illustrates the connection between first love and emotional growth. It comes from a letter written by a fifty-year-old woman, now with a comfortable home and equally comfortable marriage, which fortunately has not led her to ignore the value and place in her development which her first love holds. 'Talking to a friend the other day I was reminded of how lucky I have been. My friend was saying that she had never been in love. She is married and feels affectionate towards her husband, but freely admits that she had never been in love with him nor anyone else. I love my husband very much. It is requited and therefore happy love. Yet, my thoughts often wander to the first time that I fell in love. I know that what I have now is not quite the same nor can I expect it to be. I suspect that every woman remembers her first love as being particularly special. Like all girls I was fond of reading romances. I would indulge myself in dreams of handsome strangers sweeping me off to some far away Utopia. In reality, I would assess each new boyfriend and wait to fall in love with him. In fact it wasn't until I had outgrown this stage and become involved with activities which sublimated these young amorous desires that it actually happened to me. I literally "fell" in love. To all those writers of romantic novels whose heroines suddenly become madly in love, I say rubbish! Falling in love is a gradual process. As it takes time for a flower to unfold so it takes time to fall in love. The realisation that I was in love was certainly sudden, but I was aware that this realisation was the result of a relationship which had been growing towards this point for some time. Being in love for the first time is a period of my life which will always remain clear and complete in my memory. My naivity was indescribable. No one could have been less subtle. Once it really hit me that I was in love with someone who was in love with me, I just hit an all-time ecstasy of happiness. Looking back, I can see that I must have been a source of amusement to all my friends, as well as something of an annoyance. To be that happy means one tends to impose it on others, to demand that everyone and everything around one is in accordance and equally happy.

'I think that the mistake one makes with one's first love is that one suffocates love in its own wonder. But it is almost inevitable because it is all so wonderful, or at least I found it so. There was no need for food, nor drink nor money or anything except him and talking into the small hours, making love and talking some more and falling asleep all entwined. He provided my senses with their fill. Not being with him was a constant wish to be with him. Being with him was a constant wish for him not to go away. Walking along the street knowing it showed; this love which danced in front of us and touched passers-by so that they smiled and remembered what it had been with them and how it ended. Because we were young we would do crazy things, since love makes you disregard convention. Love isolates and protects so that the disapproval of others becomes a joke. We would laugh together because people thought us crazy. We were terribly conceited but that didn't matter too much. But first love is ephemeral and has to end. Mine ended, yet in a strange way it goes on. I cannot think of him without tenderness still. We will always have a bond even though we probably wouldn't recognise one another if we passed in the street today. I love my husband but in a more sophisticated way which better suits my mellowing years. At least unlike my friend I have known the other wilder love which accompanies youth'.

With few exceptions, the women interviewed, who were for the most part intelligent and articulate, showed greater emotional excitement and fulfilment through the love they were able to feel for another individual rather than through receiving love. Here the so-called 'natural passivity' of women comes under question. It was the active state and behaviour attributed to loving which was felt to be most enriching; not one woman could find the same depth of joy in the passive experience of being loved, (although, of course, one would not try to deny that unreciprocated love brought great unhappiness and that where love was shared there existed a more complete satisfaction). The satisfaction gained from loving probably accounts for the many incidents where women, badly treated by men and accused of weakness and passivity by relations and friends, have to reply: 'But I love him, so I must stay with him'. The woman stays so that she may go on with the emotionally satisfying experience of giving love. An unresponsive lover is preferable to no lover simply because he is *there* to be loved, he is someone towards whom love can be directed. There are many other factors involved in these cases such as masochism, guilt; almost every school of psychology provides different reasons as to why certain women love certain men. But, without this overpowering urge to love, so great that it over-rides the necessity of being loved, the numerous other factors may never manifest themselves. Sex is one of the means by which a woman can demonstrate and act out her love. Thus a man can gain a sexual hold on a woman which she finds almost impossible to resist, as in the following instance:

'At nineteen I had my first real love affair. He was thirty two, handsome and with such charm that he completely swept me off my feet. After a few weeks he persuaded me to go and live with him. At first I wasn't sure what he did for a living. I was so happy that he had so much time to spend with me. I was doing modelling work then and my time was more or less my own. He explained to me that he was a professional gambler, which covered a multitude of sins. I soon discovered that he had a second girlfriend who was a prostitute and who was supplying him with the money he was spending on me. He had such a hold on me that I felt I was in sexual bondage to him and grew to accept all the awful things I gradually learnt about him. Two or three times a week he would give me a dose of benzedrine and we would have sex all through the night until I was weak and sore, and still wanting more. When he didn't have an orgasm during these sessions there would be cunnilingus for what seemed like hours, beautiful torture, a feeling of hurting insatiability. Sometimes he would phone a friend to come and join us. Once I was 'high' on the stuff, and both men would have intercourse with me; he particularly loved to see me commit fellatio on his friends while he was having intercourse with me. After a few months he introduced a prostitute girlfriend into our sessions; she and I would make love passionately to one another for his entertainment. I have never liked women not even as friends really: I much prefer the company of men, but I developed quite a skill at making love with this woman and later with other friends he met. He tried hard to get me to take on a few select paying clients. I fought hard against it but finally succumbed; twice I did it for money but this was too much to take and I left him. I felt very low, as though life had no meaning for me'.

Can we then assume that it is necessary for a heterosexual woman to have a love object of the opposite sex? In general I think this is so remembering as always that for every rule there are the inevitable exceptions. There are those who appear to manage quite well without a particular man in their lives and others who feel that they simply do not have the capacity for giving love. The latter case was illustrated in an interview with a lonely middle-aged woman who was currently undergoing treatment for a nervous illness. The interview took place in her disturbingly neat one-roomed home in South London. Due to her illness, which had its roots in a physical disorder, her social life was non-existent. 'I can't seem to love people', she said, 'only things'. When asked to qualify the statement she was unable to do so. 'That's all there is to it', was her reply.

A Jewish widow interviewed in the similarly depressing dark atmosphere of her North London house has been searching all her life for the elusive 'male love object'. At the age of twenty-eight she married a man much older than herself, although she could not remember how much older. Their courtship lasted for eighteen months. They did not make love until their wedding night because the widow felt it was important to remain a virgin until marriage. That first night was a let-down: 'I was disappointed so I can't really describe it as enjoyable. However, I didn't find it painful so I was fortunate in that respect, but I had expected something much more exhilarating than that which I had received. All my life I have been looking for what I didn't get on that occasion'.

She came to the conclusion that her husband was 'a little impotent'. He died seven years after they were married but prior to that they had agreed to lead their separate lives. For the past twelve years the widow has been having sex with a man whom she described as her 'lover', but admits that during that time she has had sex with many other men.

'I'm not sure even after all these years', she said, 'that I really know how to make love. I am a recipient rather than a giver. I do instigate love-making, not because I want sex but because I want the man. To me sex is a weapon to be used in the battle for getting a man, who in himself is a status symbol. I get rather tired because when one has a lover sex isn't extended over an even period as in marriage; rather it happens in bouts – a lot in a little time is probably the best way of expressing my point. What most impresses me is that now, despite the fact that I am getting older, through the power of sex I can still get a man and this is marvellous. I suppose it's very wicked but it's no longer a case of whether or not I enjoy sex but of whether or not I can still get a man. Undoubtedly I am a lonely person. I can be in bed with a man and still feel lonely. The wretched man is on the other side of the bed and he might just as well not be there. It seems like two separate people lying on one bed. I never remarried simply because the men I wanted didn't want me and the men who wanted me I didn't want. The older I get the less I know what love is. At one time I used to be in and out of love every five minutes although, if one defines love as something which is lasting and which can endure all circumstances, then I am not at all sure that I have ever been in love. I want a man who will accept me totally, but I am no longer looking for that man because I know such an attainment is impossible. As for my future . . . well I'm too old to have a future. It's not as though I feel any different. I was lucky as the menopause had little effect on me. I haven't had a new man for years. I have just had the old ones time and time again. I don't know how I would stand it if I had to go onto the open market and find one. That would probably frighten me somewhat even though in the past if I wanted a new man I'd have found him'.

The widow spoke of the status symbol of a man and so touched upon one of the most crippling social attitudes. In today's world women are educated and often highly qualified. Financially they are well able to maintain themselves. Parental control diminishes at an earlier age than ever before and the young girl is free to live where and how she pleases. She no longer needs a male partner to provide her with a home nor as an escort on holidays abroad, in bars, clubs or public dance halls. In theory, socially she has no need of a man, but here again theory and reality divide. Despite the fact that she is given a formal education to equip her for a life other than motherhood the informal side of her education, gained from observation and information and interpreted from general social implications, prepares her for a role which necessitates the presence of a husband. Marriage represents the situation in which she will act out this role and without which society will regard her as an unfulfilled woman. This is, I suppose, the basic grudge of the feminists who demand equal opportunity for its own sake. Among my personal grudges against the stigma attached to the unmarried woman is that it breeds so much unhappiness within marriage. As the young girl sees her friends marry she becomes less sure of herself and more determined not to be left on the shelf. As she grows older the situation becomes more urgent, and in such a situation she is more likely to accept a proposal of marriage because she feels she might not receive another, rather than because she genuinely loves the man concerned. She will tell herself that she loves him, she will tell her friends and relations she loves him and will lose herself in her own fabrication. The marriage takes place and a few years later, somewhat battered, but not much wiser she will say in a tone of sincere surprise, 'I thought that I loved him'.

A woman caught up in this syndrome and desperate to acquire a husband, and with him an identity for herself, will blind herself to her partner's every fault or convince herself that marriage will change him. It seems almost impossible that a woman can know the man she marries for four years beforehand and after her divorce make the following statement: 'I knew from the beginning that my marriage would be disastrous. I discovered later that my husband was not only a compulsive gambler but that he also drank. I had known nothing of this. We used to go to a pub occasionally but I didn't know that he drank much'. Whether or not this situation results from the social need to have a man or from the need to possess a love object, as we have already discussed, is hard to decide. Both aspects overlap and influence one another to the extent that it is difficult to make a division. It would be interesting to see what would happen if the social pressures towards marriage were removed.

In any relationship which is insecurely based sex can play a major part in making or breaking a partnership. I would not suggest that compatability in bed is a cure for all failing marriages, but sexual incompatability and sexual problems loomed large in the cases where women interviewed were separated or divorced. A divorcee previously quoted remarked that the best time to talk to a person is after you have made love with them for then they are both open and receptive. Consequently, if a couple make love successfully, that is to the *physical* and *emotional* satisfaction of both, they have created a bond which facilitates communication on all levels. Of course one can always dispute whether one is putting the cart before the horse. It is far too black and white to state that a good sexual relationship means that other aspects of the relationship will necessarily follow suit. From a different standpoint the reverse could as well be true. A husband I once talked to explained it as possible also. He said: 'Undoubtedly sex is an important part of our relationship. Many aspects of our behaviour towards one another seem to be affected by our sex life. If we make love and it's good we don't quarrel or argue for days, we seem to come towards one another somehow. Conversely, if we make love and it isn't so good because perhaps one of us is tired, it doesn't automatically have an adverse effect on our relationship – but it can happen that way. If we have a spell without making love this seems to cause us to flirt with one another. But if we have an argument during such a period then it seems to drive us temporarily apart'.

For this husband and for most people the sexual side of marriage has some influence upon the relationship as a whole. Sex is so closely interwoven into all aspects of the relationship that if something is wrong sexually it will undoubtedly interfere with the lives of the two people, both as individuals and as a couple. Sexual compatability is not only important from the point of view of sexual satisfaction, but physical closeness in itself encourages an exchange of energy. Vanessa Redgrave, perhaps one of the most 'womanly' women of our time, was once quoted as saying: 'Physical love whether it's breastfeeding or making love or cuddling or touching or stroking or fighting is the best way of sharing an experience, of creating a relationship'. It is no coincidence that for many couples, bed is as much a place for talking as it is for making love and sleeping.

Once again our old enemy ignorance is often the root-cause of the inability to establish a satisfactory sexual relationship in marriage. When one has been brought up to regard sex as something which is never talked about it is almost impossible to find the words to communicate one's problem. Also, of course, it is impossible to discuss something of which one is not even aware.

Mrs. L. is now forty-six. She was married at nineteen, divorced at twenty-two and remarried at twenty-three. At the age of sixteen she fell in love with a boy whom she allowed to make love to her. They had sex about four or five times. Mrs. L's parents had never discussed sex with her so she had no idea what to expect, and no conception that women could gain pleasure from sex. Her first boyfriend refused to allow her to move during coitus as he was frightened that she might become pregnant if he were to experience an uncontrolled ejaculation.

'This first affair certainly had a subsequent effect on my sex-life', remarked Mrs L. during the interview, 'because during my first marriage and for part of my second, I imagined that I was frigid. Although I always enjoyed sex I felt that I should be getting something more out of it. I think that if I had had a full and proper sexual encounter the first time then I would have gone on that way'.

Her first boyfriend left her. She was terribly upset and joined the Forces as a last resort. There she met her first husband who was eight years older than herself and who appeared to her as 'very mature'. They married

39

despite opposition from parents: 'We had sex a couple of times before marriage and again, although it seemed satisfactory at the time, looking back, I knew that it wasn't. I didn't have an orgasm at all during my first marriage. I just didn't know what an orgasm was. Being older than me my husband treated me like a little girl. If I did something wrong he would tell me off like a father. He wouldn't show his disapproval until about two weeks after the event, which meant that things were always hanging over me and it became unbearable. He was sent abroad with the idea that I should follow but I decided that I would be happier without him so I never saw him again.

I met my present husband while working away from home. He was the same age and we had similar interests. I found him sexually attractive. Even now I find it is sexual attraction which draws me to certain men even for the purpose of friendship alone. I felt that sex with him was much better although I still didn't have an orgasm But it was satisfactory because we were a good match. My husband had had no previous sexual experience, but this didn't bother me as I felt that I had learnt enough from my first marriage to be able to help him over any stumbling blocks. Things were fine until the birth of my daughter. I ceased to be interested in sex. I could talk about it but I didn't want it. It wasn't until about five years later that I discovered the reason. It became apparent that I didn't really get anything out of sex because I hadn't experienced an orgasm. I discovered this through reading. I had several girlfriends at the time and mentioned it to them. One girl was extremely interested because although she had been married several years she didn't know anything about it either. Another just laughed and said she didn't know how I could have been married all that time without knowing about it. Even then I didn't know how to go about achieving an orgasm. It intrigued me to know that this girl had an orgasm each time she had intercourse. I felt that it was time to discuss the subject with my husband. We felt that my failure might be due to the fact that I wouldn't allow him to manipulate my genitals. I had never allowed him to do this before because every time he touched my clitoris I felt that I wanted to urinate. Of course, I didn't realise that this was a purely momentary feeling and that one got beyond it. One of my friends had prevented her husband from touching her clitoris for exactly the same reason. However, my husband and I experimented and found that I could reach orgasm through manual stimulation. The first time that it happened I felt so marvellous that I burst into tears. Obviously this was what I had been missing all those years. I felt that this was what married life really meant. I don't have an orgasm during intercourse, sometimes I enjoy the sensations of intercourse and sometimes not. However, by that time I have already had my orgasm so I don't mind'.

Mrs. L. is now busy making sure that present day teenagers do not find themselves in her predicament; she has become an open-minded confidante to her own young daughter and half the teenage population of the neighbourhood.

One woman blamed pre-menstrual tension as the cause of the sexual breakdown of her marriage: 'It was hopeless from the word go, but in retrospect I can see that our marriage floundered on pre-menstrual tension. I had been married for about two weeks when I got pre-menstrual tension although at the time I didn't know what it was and couldn't understand it. It made me quite schizophrenic. One minute I would be fine and the next I would be like a raving maniac, there wasn't a thing to be done about it. This of course caused arguments and we would have great difficulty in becoming friends again. By the time we did my cycle was round again. I would also have pre-menstrual tension for the two days of ovulation. This, along with the period, plus the period of five days meant that for fourteen days of each month I would be impossible to live with. I thought that I was in love with my husband, but actually I don't think that I was aware of what love was. I was excited by him simply because he was a very exciting person. There was some sort of magnetism about him. He didn't really understand my problem of pre-mentrual tension. One of the ways that I know I am in the middle of an attack is that I begin hating everyone for no reason whatsoever. Somehow this hate is always directed at those closest to me. During my marriage I wasn't interested in sex during these periods, except during ovulation when I felt a great need for it. At one stage of the pre-menstrual experience you can discuss it and the way it is affecting you, but eventually you go beyond that. Few men can understand this phenomenon. Even those who know about it and have it explained to them can never really bring themselves to understand it simply because it is so outside their personal experience.

My husband and I didn't really progress sexually, mainly because of his lack of experience and because I found it difficult to be spontaneous. I didn't want to have a child although I loved other people's children. However, I realised that I am not very practical and was really unsuitable for the responsibilities of parenthood, but nevertheless I became pregnant within three months of marriage. It was too terrible for words. I suffered from tension for the whole nine months, and when they presented me with this baby, all I wanted to do was run away from the responsibility. My husband and I lived in a furnished flat and when the landlord discovered that I was pregnant he threw us out. We lived with both sets of parents for a while which caused difficulties. Eventually my husband reached the point where he was violent with me. On one occasion, after the birth of the child, he hit me and the baby began to scream. I had been brought up in this kind of circumstance myself and I didn't want my son to experience the same. So I asked my husband to leave, which he did'.

Although there may have been factors involved in the break-up of this marriage and the subject may well be accused of rationalising her mistake by blaming pre-menstrual tension, there is little doubt that this is an affliction which is suffered in varying degrees by almost all women. If, as in this case, it is an intense and frequent experience then it is bound to affect the women's ability to cope with relationships, especially the close relationship of marriage. Insufficient research has been carried out in this field and it may well be a problem overlooked by the students of marriage-counselling and even those studying the 'baby battering syndrome'.

Research so far has resulted in theories accounting for these symptoms which range from regression with the reactivation of incest wishes to hormone imbalance, activity of the pituity gland and altered carbohydrate metabolism. Some theories consider that medication for these symptoms only has a limited relieving capacity and that the treatment should be supplemented by therapy to improve the patient's psychosexual attitudes. The chief object is that the patient should improve her self-image and feel confident of her role as mother and wife within the family, which in turn reduces emotional pressure and tension.

Perhaps this school of thought makes rather a harsh judgement accusing all women who suffer from pre-menstrual tension of an essential lack of self-acceptance, but only more research can prove or disprove. Some of the further research on the Pill may prove valuable in this direction, but research by private drug firms is more likely to produce drugs than it is an overall understanding of the problems which extreme pre-menstrual tension can cause within marriage. The previous case history can only act as a reminder to husbands that the problem exists and should be recognised. It is as much the responsiblity of the husband to come to terms with his wife's pre-menstrual tension as it is for the wife to come to terms with it herself.

Many women come to trust and love their husbands partly because they feel that they are the only ones who are in tune with their sexual and emotional needs. Those who have had experience of other men are often deeply disturbed by the lack of care and understanding which they were offered and are intensely gratified to find a man who is capable of some degree of empathy. Nancy who, as we have already heard, lost her virginity to an older man whose perceptive love-making delighted her, was shattered by the treatment she received from later partners. Apart from her husband and her first lover she has had sex with twenty-six men and had this to say about them: 'Of all the men I have had sex with, only the first and later my husband have been at all interested in my needs. As far as the rest were concerned, virility meant proving that they could have an orgasm, regardless of me. I gained the impression from most of them that the only reason they slept with a woman was to prove their own virility'.

Another young wife remarked: 'I am lucky as my husband is very much aware of my physical and psychological needs; therefore our relationship is a success. Many boyfriends before my husband appeared to be attracted to me and interested in me but I could not return their affection because they lacked skill and were all rather selfish'. A forty-six-year-old with adequate sexual experience on which to draw stated: 'It would seem that the majority of men still do not think of a woman as an equal sexual being. They realise that she is capable of an orgasm but seem to think that this will happen somewhere along the line of their own build-up to climax — usually followed a few minutes afterwards by the classic enquiry, "Are you all right?" Those who make a point of finding out how the woman most enjoys sex or finds it easiest to reach her climax are few and far between. Men underrate a woman who is willing to have sex with a man who she is not in love with. This again underlines my point about equal sexual beings. Their usual attitude is that she is cheap — afterwards. Whereas, more than likely she just wanted to be kind and was also in the mood'.

D.H. Lawrence said: 'You can't fuck without sentiment'. But it appears that either this is not so of all men, or else they find it difficult to communicate the sentiment. If a man insults her sexuality, a woman will find it hard to forgive him, as in the case of this thirty-nine-year-old woman: 'My husband complains that I am too agressive because I tend to take over. Depending on his mood he seems to find orgasm either fantastically funny or repulsive. About four years ago on three con-secutive occasions, when he began to make love to me, I began to kiss and fondle him. He hit me across the thigh and arms for attempting to fondle his penis. Since then I have never been able to entirely abandon myself to him. Mostly I push him away and he allows this. He has never had an orgasm since these incidents, but then he never seems to enjoy it the way I do. When we were first married he only wanted sex once a week and that wasn't enough for me'.

Our forty-six-year-old widow went on to make another interesting point: 'I think that the reason why so many women dry up after several years of marriage is that the husband so often uses her as an outlet for pressure which has built up within himself. Women need tenderness and reassurance that they are loved as well as desired, either passionately or otherwise. Sex between the same two people year in, year out needs a great deal of thought and understanding if it is to remain remotely akin to the early enchantment. As the man by nature is the dominant partner he will usually be the one to lead — the woman will follow. If he tries to lead her he will at least feel that love-making still matters to him and that he is interested in her as his chosen sex partner and not simply as an "outlet". I doubt whether many men out at their jobs every day realise what a drag looking after small children can be on a woman. It isn't easy to cope with all the work involved in children and a home and remain fresh and pretty. Really a woman should be understood as she is and her needs fulfilled rather than a man holding an image of what he expects her to be. A woman should also be ready to adapt herself to a man, providing it does not go completely against her nature, but in return this bending to his will should be appreciated by the male so that it is a happy and rewarding process and not martyrdom'.

In his excellent book, *Love and Orgasm* (Staples Press, London, 1967) Dr. Alexander Lowen wrote:

It takes little imagination to realise that the sexual problems of women have some relation to the double standard of morality to which they have been subjected for countless generations. What normal girl hasn't been brought up to guard herself against the sexual advances of men or to regard a seduction as a defeat of her personality? It is so much a part of our culture that we speak of a 'fallen woman' but never of a 'fallen man'. The wife who steps outside her marriage to have sexual relations is condemned; the husband is merely criticised. The young woman is shamed into sexual morality; the young man is exhorted merely to be discreet. Among their peers, the seducer is acclaimed, the seduced is pitied. Until recently the pleasure of sex has been the prerogative of the male. But the emancipation of woman has culminated in her demand for equal privileges and equal satisfaction.

The double standard reflects the relegation of women to an inferior position in Western culture. Her person has been subject to masculine domination and her personality submerged in a patriarchal culture. Simone de Beauvoir was not without justification when she described women as the 'second sex'. It has been a long uphill fight for women from the time when, under Roman Law, she was her husband's chattel, to her present freedom and dignity as an equal citizen. It required a great effort to open the door of education to her, and only recently she has been accorded the rights to vote in democratic countries. But if her struggle for recognition has been largely won in the political and social areas **it is** still in progress in the sexual area.

Thus, when a woman finds a man who engenders in her the freedom of sexual expression and encourages her to use it in every possible way, she is both happy and loving towards him

For some, both men and women, sexual variety is a necessity. There are marriages which are rich and meaningful and where extra-marital activity is rarely even thought of. However, how does a married woman cope with her own desires for a more variegated sexual diet or how does she cope with such desires in her husband? Here is how one woman cleverly managed. This is the unedited story as written down for me by the fifty-two-year-old country housewife concerned. It reads like a Maupassant imagining, but both husband and wife swear to its authentity.

'At sixteen I lost my virginity; it hurt the first time and I never enjoyed it, nor expected to, because I grew up to think that sex was something you had to let a boy do to you, or he would go off with someone else. I was glad when my boy went away, for I was scared of conceiving. In the end I was the only girl of my village school year who did not have a shotgun wedding or an illegitimate baby. At eighteen I fell in love on sight with a passing cyclist of twenty-three, who stayed the night at our farm; we corresponded, but my parents hated town chaps and in the end I ran away and lived with him. After several months my parents signed the "consent" form for our marriage. My husband was not then in love with me, he wanted someone to sleep with and cook. At first we used a washable French letter, which was like a car inner tube. After it burst he pushed me, fainting with fright, into a birth control clinic. I hold the Family Planning Association record. I wore a Dutch Cap from the age of eighteen to forty-nine. Our early marriage was spoilt by the belief that sex weakened the male and so we had it only four times a week, and by a sex manual which told us that the couple failed if the woman didn't have an orgasm. I now know that I will never come more than two or three times a month. My husband recognises the symptoms and gives me a tremendous screwing, but for the rest of the time I just co-operate with him and allow him to "use me as a slave", and we both enjoy it. I just don't believe that more than a handful of women come every time they have sex, unless they only get it infrequently. I am certain that the best approach to sex for the woman is always to provide her man's needs; if he is considerate he will ensure that she enjoys it too. My husband studied day and night to get himself to college and thus for two years I endured 'domestic service', which was really slavery, but I earned his eternal gratitude and thirty pounds a year! We waited seven years to have our first child, and had two more at four and a quarterly intervals. I was always mad to have kids, he was not so keen. We struck a bargain that if he would agree to having a child I would agree to him having a mistress. It worked out very well, I was free to carry, bear and rear the child, and I knew by then that I was the only one he really loved. The mistresses knew it too, they used to get angry and walk out, the heartcry of the "other" woman—"But I shall never be the one to iron his shirts". They could be expensive, pernickety and bloody-minded, and he used to swear "never again", until my next baby, and then....

'One marvellous discovery was made during this period; I was cursed with small breasts, but feeding each infant for nine months gave me a superb pair, and I used to feed my husband too! After my last, when I was thirty-six, he kept me in milk for four years. Towards the end it was a dribble, but at first it was such that he had quite a feed. Over the years our sex-life was regular but mundane; we only used the missionary position until we discovered "spoons" (lying together sideways, woman sitting in man's lap) which is good for a quickie and you go to sleep still joined. If I was in a mood to be roused he would take me while still moist from "her", or describe in detail what they had been up to. I was proud of the fact that he had such a wonderful attraction for stubborn intellectual virgins who seem to reach breaking point as thirty looms up. Apart from odd, unsatisfactory adventures, I was always faithful, except when my husband was in the army when he encouraged me to have a married man for my physical need. With kids in the house there is no hope of fancy sex, but as two of ours left home and the youngest began to go out more my husband, by then fifty-six and still passionate, came to demand more variety. I had long worn fancy lingerie to please him but I must confess that my early chapel upbringing had conditioned me for life to be more prudish than I would wish. I can never bring myself to walk around the house without knickers, nor reach orgasm in any other than the missionary position. However, about a year ago, after thirty-two years of marriage we broke through. My husband spoke of taking another mistress and in his age group there are hoards of presentable and desperate widows. But neither of us really wanted this, so I agreed to try a new idea.

'I would submit to his demands, unusual positions, unusual entrances, unusual times, and do my best to satisfy him as a job of work. He would pay me on a fixed scale according to the service rendered and the time taken, always putting the money on the mantlepiece in the regular way. It has worked splendidly. I am several pounds a week better off for work that I enjoy, while he feels he has two women, a wife and a mistress, under his own roof. We call my earnings 'prostitution money' and already I have brought myself a few luxuries, while he is busy spurning the advances of the divorced headmistress up the road!'

Such behaviour may of course shock many people. The idea of a wife being paid for her favours goes against the moral grain of our society. Indeed even ancient societies would have frowned upon such activity; concubines were provided for the satisfaction of such urges. However I find it a refreshing story insomuch as here is a woman determined to make her husband happy and obviously enjoying the 'naughtiness' of it all. Two people are happy and convention is gladly thrown to the wind. It is an extension of a remark made by another woman during the survey: 'The first wife of Bertrand Russell was wont to take off her wedding ring and also be his lover. She had the right idea'.

Among those interviewed the general attitude towards extra-marital affairs on the part of husbands was extremely tolerant. Whether or not this is a result of 'the double standard doctrine' is hard to say but if so it is probably one of the few beneficial factors resulting from it. However, in many cases, the women declared their wish to know and in fact share their husband's extra-marital affairs, through being given description of his sexual activities with the other woman. It was the secrecy and deceit so often involved in these affairs which women found distasteful. Others said that it would cause them to look at themselves and wonder what it was they were failing to give their husbands that he could find in another woman.

Among the interviewees was a wife in whom devotion and fidelity to her husband was pronounced. She mixed in semi-intellectual circles, which had an obvious influence on her without submerging entirely her own strong personality. She was always upset by her husband's infidelity and almost felt guilty about feeling this way. 'I have tried to explain it to myself because I know that he loves me and we have what I consider a successful sex-life. I have tried to see it from his point of view, because obviously he needs variety. I am sure that a man is capable of having sex with someone in a way that is purely physical, but that same man can also have an intensely emotional relationship with another woman'.

A similar study to this one was made in France and first published in 1960 by the French Institute of Public Opinion. When asked if they thought it was excusable for a married man to have a short casual affair with another woman, fifty per cent of the French women answered in the affirmative and ten per cent said they didn't know. Thirty-five per cent of the married women under thirty-five felt that at some time all men deceive their wives and thirty-eight per cent of the married women over thirty-five felt the same. When asked what a wife should do if she discovers that her husband is deceiving her, only five per cent suggested that she should leave him. The majority, at twenty-five per cent, said that she should close her eyes to it. Twenty per cent said that she should be diplomatic, seventeen per cent that she should forgive him, sixteen per cent that she should talk it over with him, six per cent that she should reproach him, seven per cent that she should deceive him to get even. Another six per cent remarked that she should become more affectionate and charming and seven per cent gave no answer. (The total is greater than a hundred per cent because some women gave more than one answer).

Dr. Alfred Kinsey in his famous American report stated: *(Sexual Behaviour in the Human Female,* Indiana University, 1953)

It is particularly notable that the males rated their wives' extra-marital activities as prime factors in their divorces twice as often as the wives made such an evaluation of their husbands' activities. Some fifty-one per cent of the males considered that their wives' non-marital relationships had been chief factors in precipitating the divorces, and another thirty-two per cent considered them factors of some importance. Only seventeen per cent considered them minor factors. In contrast to this the females considered that the husbands' extra-marital activities were prime factors in only twenty-seven per cent of the divorces, moderate factors in forty-nine per cent and minor factors in a full twenty-four per cent. It may be a fact that the male's extra-marital activities do not do so much damage to a marriage, or the wives may be more tolerant of their husband's extra-marital relations, or the wife may not comprehend the extent to which the male activities are actually affecting the stability of their marriages. Conversely, like the true mammal that he is, the male shows himself to be more disturbed and jealous and more ready to take drastic action if he discovers that his wife is having extra-marital relations.

These data once again emphasize the fact that the reconciliation of the married individual's desire for coitus with a variety of sexual partners, and the maintenance of a stable marriage, presents a problem which has not been satisfactorily resolved in our culture. It is not likely to be resolved until man moves more completely away from his mammalian ancestry.

However, group sex, not such a new phenomenon but one which is growing rapidly in frequency and rather more slowly in acceptance, is one way in which some couples solve the problem. They feel that it lessens the danger inherent in preventing the development of emotional relationships and threatening the marriage; they feel that it is an erotic stimulant and, if successfully carried out, proof of a close and balanced relationship. A few such cases arose during the survey. One couple concerned included one other man in their bed rather than another couple. The following is an account of the relevant history described by the woman, who is a thirty-nine-year-old housewife and receptionist living in London. Her upbringing was typically middle-class, disturbed only by her father's heavy drinking.

'Up until meeting my husband, I slept with such a lot of boys that I can't really remember how many. Sex was all I wanted. Then I met my husband. He was in the same state as I was. I was seventeen and he was nineteen. He was slightly more innocent than me. He had had a domineering mother and I think that he felt guilty about sex. It was Providence that we met because if I had married a cold man I would have stuck a knife in his back and if my husband had married a frigid woman he would probably have strangled her. In spite of our being highly-sexed we didn't start having sex immediately. This seems crazy after all that had gone on before. Why we didn't fall into bed straight away I shall never know. We used to go out together all day. Neither of us worked and we used to tell the most awful lies to my parents. When I finally had sex with him I found that it was very different from the sex that I had had previously. It was as though I had just been playing around with the other men, while this was the real thing. We walked around in a daze. I don't think that at that age I was in love — except that perhaps I was in love with love and sex. I used to have orgasms practically the moment he touched me. Prior to meeting me, my husband had had sex only with prostitutes, yet with me he was terribly sensitive. We went on having sex and eventually decided to get married. When we were first married we would go to bed for two days at a time and never get up, not even to eat. We would have sex, then rest and then have more sex. However, we have been married for some time now and there came a point when we decided that we had been having the same kind of sex ever since we were kids and that we needed an extra stimulus. Consequently our sex life is now different from when we were young. We usually need a third person in order to enjoy our sex, because after a time we get bored with the same person and want a change. However, it is always another man. My husband likes to watch while the other man makes love to me. He also likes to have sex with me after someone else has had an orgasm inside me. It's something that once you start and have enjoyed it is difficult to stop. It is not easy to find men who will agree to this, but on the other hand London is full of very sexy men.

'It began one night when we went to the cinema. We were both a little drunk. I sat next to a man who put his hand up my skirt. He got me interested and before we knew what was happening the three of us were in a pub having drinks. When we came home it all started. What happens now is that my husband will watch while the other man makes love to me and then he will get into bed with us. I kiss the other man's penis while my husband is inside me and vice versa. That's about all. We sometimes get very strong-minded and decide we will just be on our own. But then we get irritable and bored. This is not because we are unhappy together, but because we have had so much sex in our lives and tried everything there is to try that I suppose normal sex gets a bit mundane, so we have something more exciting. I still enjoy having sex alone with my husband, but at weekends we have just got to change our diet. We never have another woman with us because my husband is not keen on the idea, although I wouldn't mind. I get excited by the thought of an orgy with lots of people, but my husband is basically a shy man and I don't think that he would enjoy it. I feel that whatever a man and a woman choose to do together can never be considered perverted, providing that neither party is hurt in any way. I would never have an affair with another man nor have sex with another man when my husband wasn't there. It wouldn't be worth the effort. My husband and I always do everything together. I believe that if couples experimented in bed and tried everything their marriages would be better. So many people have rows over sex and to me this is pointless. I think that my husband and I have a successful marriage'.

Undoubtedly the major attraction of group sex for women is that they are able to experience other men sexually without the deceit and conflicting loyalties involved in an affair. Even those women who were not involved with group activities felt that to deceive their husbands was the worst crime they could commit against themselves and their relationship. 'I couldn't imagine having a secret affair. I don't feel that I've missed anything sexually and a relationship with another man would only cause complications in my marriage. If I ever felt compulsively attracted to another man I think that I might have to have him before I got him out of my system, but I'd feel compelled to tell my husband about it. I hope this never does happen', was one comment.

Young and old felt alike that the extra-marital affair was wrong, but with their husband's consent or presence, it was permissible if desired. This twenty-one-year-old wife explained: 'I feel that extra-marital affairs are very wrong. I could never have an affair with another man—I would hate all the deceit and lies. I have tried group sex and enjoyed it very much. We began by taking photographs and showing them to another couple. We then progressed to taking photographs of one another and having sex with woman. He would also like to see how I get on with another man. One of the things about swapping which appeals to me is knowing that my husband would be enjoying himself. I would also find it interesting to have sex for the sake of sex. I must say that I'm not absolutely sure; it may be a good thing for our marriage if we were to swap, it may make it more exciting'.

There are, of course, women to whom the thought of group sex is abhorent: 'I dislike the idea of wife-swapping', said one seemingly liberal middle-aged wife. 'Even the term is derogatory. No one talks of husband-swapping as if a man were a piece of property. If they were to call it "marital exchange" I might come to like the idea a little more. Although, really I like to keep spouse and lovers apart, then comparison and jealousy is less likely to appear. As far as one big jolly sex party is concerned — ugh! It would be like everyone eating off the same plate'. There are many psychiatrists today who might maintain that eating off the same plate would in fact be a therapy, a way in which people might share an experience more definitely than by simply sitting down to a separate meal together. It is not an easy fact for some to grasp, but an increasing number of women are viewing this activity as a step further towards fuller self-expression and emancipation.

We have seen in this chapter how women behave and react to marriage and to love. Their diversity is such that the certainties of one are the uncertainties of another — a human rather than an entirely feminine condition.

4 Orgasm

The ultimate fulfilment of all sexual acts is the release of increased tension through orgasm. For some it is the profoundest and most mystical experience they know; for others it is a long-sought-after goal and the cause of permanent frustration. Apart from the insight and, at times the ecstatically religious experience that orgasm can provide, it is now known to be necessary both from a somatic and psychological point of view.

Primarily, orgasm is a motor reaction which takes place after a certain amount of sexual stimulation. The frequency and intensity of the orgasm will vary from occasion to occasion in each individual and, indeed, from one individual to another. Sigmund Freud was the first to impress upon Occidentals that the libido is an energy force. In 'Three Essays on Sexuality', (*Standard Edition of the Complete Psychological Works,* London, 1953) he wrote: 'we distinguish this *libido* in respect of its special origin from the *energy* which must be supposed to underlie mental process in general'. Later during his own lifetime, Freud was followed by Wilhelm Reich who, although diverting from Freud in certain aspects, grasped the full implications of the 'energy' which Freud stressed as a fundamental concept in psychoanalysis. By 1923 Reich's researches brought him to formulate the 'orgasm theory'. He felt that until this time sexologists had been aware only of potency in the capacity for ejaculation and erection. Reich considered the erection of the penis and clitoris, and male ejaculation as 'nothing but indispensable prerequisites for orgasmic potency'. Orgasmic potency he described as 'the capacity to surrender to the flow of biological energy without any inhibition; the capacity for complete discharge of all damned up sexual excitation through involuntary pleasurable contractions of the body'.

Reich's 'biological energy' is a combination of somatic and psychic energy. He added that, in the absence of inhibitions, the course of the sexual process from erectile excitement to post-orgasm relaxation in the woman is in no way different from that in the man. This statement has since been corroborated in the amazing laboratory research of the Americans, W.H. Masters and V.A. Johnson who recorded their findings in *Human Sexual Response* (London, 1966). They were able to trace a cycle of orgiastic response in both men and women which they split into four phases: the excitement phase, the plateau phase, the orgasmic or orgasm phase and the resolution or recovery phase. In each phase the pattern was similar, allowing, of course, for obvious anatonomical differences. In the orgasmic phase it was discovered in both men and women that sensations occurring in the genital organs were accompanied by changes in pulse rate, blood pressure and breathing rate.

The two women in this survey, who at the time of interview were suffering from an inability to experience orgasm have already been mentioned, as has the case of the woman who for many years of her marriage was unable to experience orgasm through fear of urination when experiencing clitoral stimulation. We have also already touched upon cases where women's emotional reaction to their partner influenced whether or not they had orgasms. However, among women who felt that they had no personal problem as far as coming to orgasm was concerned, there were mixed feelings as to their reaction on occasions when sexual relations did *not* lead to orgasm as happened sometimes in the cases of most women. Some revealed that it left them frustrated and annoyed, while others, who proved to be the majority, felt that it mattered little.

I noticed that the more balanced and mature the woman the less likely she was to be perturbed by lack of orgasm on occasions. These women had assessed their own orgasmic capacity and providing that the frequency of experience remained stable they were content with it. Susan, who was twenty, seemed somewhat emotionally shallow, as though she had never made contact with her real self nor the real self of any of the superficial young men whom she chose for her sexual partners. 'If I don't have an orgasm', she said, 'I feel totally dissatisfied and a little resentful towards the man'. Another single girl, aged twenty-three remarked that if she didn't have an orgasm during sex she felt flat as if she had been left hanging in mid-air, restless, frustrated and unsatisfied. A young wife reported that she once lived with a man whom she 'didn't really like very much, but felt sorry for'. His failure to satisfy her led her to retire to the bathroom once he had fallen asleep where she would masturbate in order to relieve herself.

Of course, feelings of resentment towards the partner may often be justified; 'I must admit that I have sometimes felt resentment', said a married twenty-one-year-old with a great deal of pre-marital sexual experience, 'but I think that the resentment was more against the fact that the man concerned didn't seem to be interested in giving me anything, but only in taking what he wanted'. For the single girl, orgasm during sexual relations may be more important simply because for her intercourse is not always regular and available when she feels most desire. This twenty-one-year-old American girl, in describing he need for orgasm, touched upon this point: 'There are times when, if I have been without sex for any length of time, I get very nervous and almost have an orgasm through riding in a taxi. I mean, it begins to preoccupy me, but at such times it's not just the sex I need, but the affection and lots of other things which manifest themselves physically, so that I feel almost on the brink of orgasm just sitting there! It's at these times that I think 'Oh God! Just anyone'. But if I do meet someone whom I find sexually attractive and whom I know feels the same about me, I find that I still go through the whole social bit and the former feelings begin to dissipate'.

Many of the married women who felt satisfied with their sex lives did not count it essential to have an orgasm every time they and their husbands made love; conversely they did seem to feel it essential for their husbands. The following quotation is taken from the interview of a worldly young wife whose relationship with her husband constituted one of the soundest marriages I encountered: 'I don't always achieve orgasm, but I certainly reach peaks of intense pleasure whenever we have sex, but I must admit that it is the final orgasm which is so enthralling. I can obtain great pleasure from helping my partner towards orgasm without actually reaching a climax myself. Perhaps this is because during the month I have my fair share of orgasms. Sometimes if I don't have an orgasm I feel a little pent up and restless but this doesen't happen often'.

A housewife who, at the age of twenty-one, was well content with marriage and family life, and taught in Sunday School, remarked on the subject: 'On the occasions when I have failed to have an orgasm I have felt flat. Not depressed or anything, but as if I had left a job unfinished. I find compensation if my husband has had a climax, but we do not usually finish intercourse until both of us has had an orgasm. I am lucky because my husband can carry on after his orgasm if I have not had mine'. A number spoke of the joy and excitement they could gain from the orgasm of the man they loved: 'Sometimes', said a twenty-two-year-old, who had been married for a year, 'my husband will become terribly excited and quite unable to control himself. He always feels some regret on these occasions because he has not given me time for my orgasm I have tried to explain to him that he cannot be considered to suffer from premature ejaculation as he so often satisfies me, and that at these times I get as much pleasure from the joy of his uncontrolled excitement as from an orgasm of my own experience'.

A few women spoke of how they were capable of leading themselves to orgasm mainly through the movements of their own bodies or through directing their partners. A thirty-three-year-old married woman made a special point of describing her technique for ensuring her orgasm: 'I feel that orgasm is important in a sexual relationship for both partners, but it doesn't have to happen every time. If I can obtain one orgasm a week then I am satisfied. However, I do feel that when a woman indicates to her partner that she has a strong desire for sex then it is most important that she be brought to a climax. On occasions when I make the first overtures in sex play, as soon as my husband is fully aroused, I quickly roll on top of him and take on the dominant role. Once his penis has penetrated me then I perform the movements normally made by the male partner until I finally achieve orgasm. I have had some of my most satisfying climaxes in this manner'.

I am sure that the majority of women take an active part in bringing about their orgasm but most refuse to consider it because they like to feel that their orgasm has been induced purely by the man – that it is a 'gift' from him. There is of course a residue of the feeling that orgasm in the female is not quite nice. 'I'm sure it must be horrible to see', said one woman when describing her physical reactions during orgasm. I have seen case histories where women stated that they had an orgasm 'despite themselves'. Such a woman may wish to feel that she had no part in bringing about the phenomenon and that the responsibility lies entirely with her partner – an attitude directly in opposition to that of the woman who may convincingly simulate orgasm.

In the same way that women want their man to have an orgasm, because they then feel that they have helped him towards fulfilment, some women realise that for the sensitive male the same thing applies in reverse. There have been cases when the simulation of orgasm on the part of a woman has merely led to prolongment of a sexual problem and in one case I know of it led to divorce, but this is usually when orgasm is always simulated and never real. I interviewed one woman who was honest enough to admit that sometimes she pulled this trick, something which I feel few women would admit to. 'Very often, we make love', she said, 'and I don't have an orgasm, but it's his closeness and the meaning of sex that matters to me. Sometimes I tell him I've come when I haven't, because in some way I feel that I would be letting him down; or perhaps I feel I have to live up to a sort of sexy image I have created of myself in my mind'.

This brings us to the great orgasm myth, one of the less beneficial results of the sexual emancipation of women. In America, writers and sexologists have already coined the cynical expression 'Big O' to parody the growing obsession with female orgasm. It seems that attitudes to sexual behaviour are most often manifested in extremes. From the time when women were not supposed to enjoy sex but expected to consider it a wifely duty carried out with the stoicism with which they scrubbed the floors, we have come, rather rapidly, to a time when all women are expected to experience orgasm if only as an assertion of femininity. To an extent the cause of this lies in public interpretations of the crop of marriage and sex manuals published over the past twenty-five years which quite rightly call for due consideration for women. Also to blame is the current fashion for acquiring at least a superficial knowledge of psychology in order to pass as 'educated' at middle-class intelligensia social gatherings.

It is common to speak of 'achieving', 'reaching' or 'attaining' orgasm and of 'failure' to do so. These words have, in fact, become so common that they mean the same as 'having an orgasm' or 'not having an orgasm', but initially they were no doubt taken literally, and the connotation remains. Thus, preoccupation with female orgasm has added to the long list of the neuroses of our time. It is a difficult subject to discuss because undoubtedly orgasm is biologically necessary and as much the right of women as of men, but as with anything else preoccupation can only lead to false emphasis. There are women who for both psychological and physical reasons do not come to orgasm immediately, frequently and without patience. Some women have been led to believe that to have sex without orgasm is tantamount to admitting that they are lacking in femininity, 'not proper women'. Their frantic strivings to attain the womanly goal act as a blockage to experiencing that which they so covet.

Although only twenty, one single girl interviewed had already realised the dangers inherent in the 'Big O' attitude: 'I can see it is important that during sexual intercourse a woman does have orgasm but people should not become obsessed with the idea. Orgasm in its intensity and frequency is unique, just as every person is unique. It could happen that with the present obsession with female orgasm people may feel they have failed themselves and one another if the incidence is not frequent nor the experience soul-shaking. This would be very wrong. The concentration on orgasm could overshadow, or even obliterate in people's minds all the rest of what sex is about — the intimacy, warmth, sensations and the sheer delight of being so close to another human being whom you love'. As this girl suggests, and I believe rightly so, that orgasm is a unique and personal experience, let us examine the descriptions I received from some of the women interviewed.

'Describe an orgasm', is quite a formidable request; many declined to do so on the grounds that their powers of description were inadequate, some tried at the same time, reminding me that I had dropped on them a demand which they hardly felt able to fulfill. A rigidity of all parts of the body was frequently described as the onset of orgasm and changes of temperature were often mentioned — some went hot, some cold. Said one woman, aged thirty-nine, about to part from her husband and already involved in a relationship with another man: 'Just before an orgasm my hair seems to burn and stand on end like a gollywog, my fingernails burn, my breasts feel like volcanoes that are about to erupt'. 'It begins at the pit of my stomach', remarked a twenty-three-year-old New Zealander. 'It spreads upwards but it is most intense at the pit of my stomach'.

Most agreed that the factors which produce orgasm are a combination of the physical and psychological, although a few felt them to be more overtly physical. After one year of marriage twenty-three-year-old Yvonne felt: 'Orgasm is most certainly a combination of physical and psychological factors, but not an equal combination. I find that I have to be psychologically predisposed to sexual play before I can successfully indulge. However, there is a point where my psychological disposition is irrelevant, i.e. when approaching orgasm; then it is essentially a physical thing. Any psychological interaction at this time is an embellishment. On these occasions orgasm is more profound and cannot simply be described as pleasure'.

'For me orgasm comes in big waves', said a twenty-one-year old, also quite recently married. 'I can see the waves getting bigger and bigger, until eventually there comes a wave which is so big I can't ride it. The subsequent waves become gentler and gentler until it is peaceful again. My husband tells me that I have violent orgasms which last a comparatively long time. I have found that since the birth of my child orgasms are greater in intensity. Orgasm is for me mostly a physical thing, although some-times I feel it as being psychological. On a few rare occasions my husband and I have been aware of a great spiritual union, but it is exceptional for this to happen. I think in a well-adjusted person orgasm should be both physical and psychological, but I wouldn't call myself well-adjusted. Obviously orgasm fulfills a deep psychological need'.

That orgasm varies in sensation was confirmed by the following two women, whose descriptions are almost identical. The first is Danish, aged thirty-seven: 'It is not always the same feeling. It goes from a sort of lovely gentle feeling to a great big marvellous explosion where one becomes almost unconscious'. The second is a forty-six-year-old widow: 'Orgasm varies from a pleasant feeling, gently engulfing and relaxing, to a pleasure-pain, which completely exhausts me'.

Visual images are common: 'It takes over my whole body and my mind seems to float. Everything goes intensely purple with white lights. I experience the most marvellous feeling of complete being. I don't think that I could ever feel more completely alive'.

'Melting', 'floating' and 'explosion' were three words repeatedly used in the descriptions. Life-death images were also used. 'During an orgasm it wouldn't matter to me if I died', was one example. This analogy comes out particularly strongly in the description of one girl: 'The first time that we made love I thought that I was going to die there and then because that was what life was all about and there wasn't much else to touch beyond it. I had never had an orgasm before and in fact for quite a while I went on having orgasms without knowing what they were. As far as I was con-cerned it was a magical experience which was induced through the spell of him. It's impossible to describe orgasm adequately, especially the times when it is most intense, because words are tainted by all sorts of con-notations. However, I'll try. It is as if you are filled with the music which you share with all living things; as if the spirit of all that has lived, does live or will ever live, passes through you. It's an affirmation that you are holy'.

A precise description was furnished by a thirty-nine-year-old married pharmacist: 'Orgasm varies in intensity depending on factors such as health, fatigue and the time of the month. During an intense orgasm one loses all sense of time and space. Initally, I feel a pulsating inside me stemming from just below the navel. My breasts tingle and I am told that my nipples stand erect. I feel that I want to touch my partner with the whole of my body surface, inside and out. If he manages to touch the hypersensitive spot I presume to be the cervix then it is painful, but at the same time I shiver all over with ecstasy. If, for instance, I am bending over the arm of a chair, I am liable to lose all sense of balance. I cannot see in the sense that I no longer bother to focus my eyes. Sounds become quite meaningless. I try to eat him alive. I sometimes remember afterwards that I was banging my head against a wall or rolling my head from side to side. Suddenly I feel completely exhausted, disjointed, just as if I am a person who has melted into thin air. In this state I find almost complete absence of feeling. I am in a dream-like state from which it takes me an unknown time to recover'.

When Kinsey published his controversial *Sexual Behaviour in the Human Female*, he was derided for believing the fourteen per cent of women interviewed who spoke of experiencing multiple orgasm. The unbelievers, mostly men, felt that the women were referring to minor climaxes which they mistook for complete orgasm. Two doctors, E.B. Bergler and W.S. Kroger, went so far as to write a book, *Kinsey's Myth of Female Sexuality* (New York, 1954), in which they rejected all possibility of multiple orgasm. However, Masters and Johnson, whose research was a direct progression from Kinsey's findings, were later to observe multiple orgasm in their women volunteers both during intercourse and masturbation. Remembering the anatomy of orgasm, the four stages which I mentioned earlier, it is not difficult to understand the biological principles behind multiple orgasm. After the resolution phase the woman returns to the plateau phase and if stimulation continues she may be able to reach the orgasmic phase again; unlike the male she does not have to reconstruct the entire pattern of sexual response from the excitement phase.

Some of the women in this study were able to report experience of multiple orgasm while for others it was an unknown experience. Those who did have multiple orgasm did not do so every time they had sex. All the women considered themselves satisfied with one orgasm during lovemaking. The general feeling was that the multiple experience was intense but not necessary. For such experience is likely to lead to total sexual exhaustion. A forty-two-year-old teacher told me: 'I am capable of having more than one orgasm during intercourse, but three is about my limit because then I begin to get tired'.

'Usually after the first orgasm I don't want any more', said a twenty-one-year-old, 'it really depends on my partner. I think that the first orgasm is always the best, after that I begin to get a bit uncomfortable. If I'm not given a rest I find it difficult to reach another'.

Another medically controversial point in the issue of female sexual response is clitoral versus vaginal orgasm. As I see it, this distinction is only relevant to medical science at present. After all it matters little where the source of orgasm lies. However, it is possible that because many women do not know the important part played in orgasmic response by the thousands of nerve endings of the clitoris, they may never experience orgasm.

Freud first propounded the theory differentiating the nature of the vaginal orgasm from the clitoral orgasm when he stated that little girls, after discovering that they can obtain orgasm through self-stimulation of the clitoris, must as women transfer attention to the vagina. I believe that once a woman has discovered the best means of realising sexual satisfaction, has conveyed this to her partner and is happy with the result, then she should turn a deaf ear to all the various theories. For some women the thought that they might not come to orgasm through stimulation of the vagina, that most symbolic of female and life symbols, is psychologically disturbing. These people are likely to consider themselves as 'not quite women' and 'rather unnatural'. It is sad that our culture has forced on women such an intense need to prove their own femininity to themselves. If any woman reading this is worried by the fact that she does not think her orgasms 'vaginal', then I advise her to forget it and enjoy what she has got; the clitoris after all is as much a part of the female genitalia as the vagina. When some women say that they cannot have a vaginal orgasm, what they really mean is that they cannot have an orgasm through intercourse, but only through manual or oral stimulation. Again, the psychological effect is obvious, and one can sympathise with such a woman who dearly wishes to experience orgasm through penetration by the man she loves. There may be many reasons for this: orgasm-anxiety and subconscious fears of penetration or resentment towards penetration have proved material for whole psycho-analytical text books. Briefly one can only give the advice that obsession with such a desire will almost certainly prevent all likelihood of its fulfilment, and also that manual stimulation and penile penetration are possible at the same time.

Orgasm is a total experience not only of oneself but of one's partner. It is the closest a woman can come to being a man and the closest a man can come to becoming a woman. Any man who wishes that a woman should be enriched through his making love to her will want to ensure that she knows orgasm.

5 Lesbianism and Deviation

Homosexuals, male and female, have come to be one of the groups which the self-styled 'normal' people of the world are apt to refer to collectively as 'them', and at whom some of the most misinformed criticism is directed. Because black and white are the least complicated colours in which to paint the world, there is a cultural insistence that women should be feminine, men should be masculine and then we shall all know where we stand.

Thus, those who confuse the issue by committing the heinious crime of physically desiring a member of their own sex are made to pay for their sins by becoming the target of ridiculous jokes and social ostracism. It is all very well in the patchwork world of show business (the public do not want ordinary stars) but not in our factory/street/school/church. The endless psychiatric theories concerning the development of homosexuality have to a certain extent defeated their purpose. They may have enlightened a few, but for the most part, thrown out superficially as they are through mass media, theories concerning hatred and rejection of the mother, or of the father, the parent's wish for a child of a different sex, narcissistic mothers, etc., have only caused confusion, not understanding. The very fact that psychiatrists study homosexuality has left the masses with the conclusion that whatever else they may be, the male or female homosexual is unquestionably disturbed.

The homosexual might well be disturbed, but his or her disturbance may be as easily traced to the frustrated need to fit into an antagonistic community as much as it may be directly connected to childhood experiences. Self-acceptance is the ultimate problem facing a member of any minority group. Once a person has become totally aware of himself and has wholly accepted himself then he becomes a little less sensitive to non-acceptance by a major section of the society in which he lives. However, the two are so correlated that it is an exceptional person who may achieve the former without the latter. People tend to judge themselves as they are repeatedly judged by others. Consequently, if a woman meets with hostility, suspicion and disdain, when her lesbian inclinations are revealed to her heterosexual contacts, she will find the process of self-acceptance painful and perhaps impossible. Unless such a woman finds among friends and relatives an understanding which is not patronising, she may well become the self-assertive, aggressive character, permanently on the defensive, which has become the image of the 'typical' lesbian. In reality, such behaviour is less typical of a particular sexual orientation, but rather typical of any human being who is derided by others for possessing what are to her, her most tender and precious feelings.

Before examining the four interviews with exclusively homosexual women which formed part of this study, it may be appropriate to detail the homosexual experiences of a number of women who are, to all intents and purposes, predominantly heterosexual. Kinsey found that a quarter of his female sample had recognised erotic response to other females by the time they had reached the age of thirty. A further nineteen per cent of his sample had had specifically sexual contacts with other females by the time they had reached the age of forty.

The extent and depth to which a predominantly heterosexual woman will allow her homosexual relationships to move depends on her sense of ability to cope with the situation. Usually such a woman will set a limitation — by using the criterion that the homosexual relationship should not be allowed to inhibit her heterosexual outlets, as for example, in the case of her homosexual partner becoming possessive or over-demanding. The initiation of the lesbian liaison may be premediated and the result of an unsavoury experience with a man, such as in the case of forty-two-year-old Mrs S, a well educated and much travelled woman of the world. 'Once while living in France I did have an affair with a woman because I was terrified of becoming pregnant. I had a nasty scare in Norway where I was having an affair with a Norwegian man. There is one thing that Norwegian men are not keen on and that is contraception, chiefly because it costs money. They use coitus interruptus and I don't think that they are very good at that. This scare turned me off sex with men for a long time. I met my girlfriend in a café in Paris which is specially for women. I thought that I would like a girlfriend because I needed sex, but at the same time I didn't want a man. I knew that there were such cafés in Paris, so I went along to one. However, sex with a woman is much less complete than sex with a man specially if one of the women is trying to be a man, which was the case with my girlfriend. She became terribly possessive and jealous about my relationships with other people, men or women, so I gave her up. Now that I am married I think that I could still be attracted to a woman, but it would worry me because I would feel that I was being unfaithful to my husband'.

Mrs B., a forty-five-year old former actress, also called a halt to her lesbian relationship when it began to surpass certain limits: 'My affair was with a woman who lived upstairs from me when I was between my second and third marriages. One night she came downstairs frightened out of her wits because a man had tried to break into her flat. We had a few drinks and I asked her if she wanted to stay the night because of what had happened. She agreed and we went to bed. I was drowsy and fell asleep. The next thing I knew I woke up and she was kissing my breasts, I was dumbfounded. Then she started to kiss me all over. I was terribly embarrassed. She began to cry because I wouldn't let her make love to me. I said, "I don't know what you want so I can't do anything back to you". She said that she didn't want me to do anything; she just wanted to make love to me. So I thought – why not? In the end I quite enjoyed it. I had several orgasms and they were no different to when I was with a man. I let her make love to me several times after that. Once we had a threesome with one of my boyfriends. I was embarrassed at first but once I got over that I had a ball. I think that he was dreadfully embarrassed because afterwards he said that we must never do it again . Eventually my girfriend wanted to use a dildo on me. I couldn't bear that. I was rather disgusted and thought – this is not me, I'm a man's woman'.

A twenty-six-year-old West Indian girl, who had an isolated homosexual relationship, fell for the gentleness of love-making from another woman: 'We were introduced and she just liked me so it happened. She made love to me and I enjoyed it. I made love in response to her because I was fond of her. We made love every week for a few months and through this I came to the conclusion that women definitely have an understanding of one another's sexual needs. This girl was bi-sexual and I couldn't see either of us ending up as exclusively lesbian. I don't go out and look for girls but I suppose if I liked someone it could happen again. During love-making with my girlfriend I would always come to orgasm. She would kiss my genitals and that more or less automatically gives me an orgasm. We would kiss and I would respond to her. I think that I received more tenderness from her than I have ever had from any man. I think that men use women'.

A forty-six-year-old housewife and mother of two teenage daughters reporting on her lesbian contacts also stressed the aspect of gentle love-making. 'I'm not attracted to members of my own sex, but on two occasions attractive women have made advances to me. On each occasion I wanted the experience and found it enjoyable, tender and sad. It was enjoyable from a physical standpoint because gentleness in caressing is just what I love. I can't explain the sadness. I feel that I could never form a true lesbian partnership, it could only ever be a pleasant diversion, an isolated incident'.

Lisa was another who, although she felt that she was not attracted to members of her own sex, had had encounters which contained elements of homosexuality. 'I once went to a lesbian bar and this fat blonde started talking to me and dancing with me. I was curious to see what it was like, so we went back to my apartment. It wasn't very interesting and I didn't have an orgasm. I think my curiosity stems from when I left home and met a girl who had a tremendous influence on me. I didn't know for some time that she was homosexual. She was very neurotic and would throw fits. I would have to go over to her flat and she always wanted to go to sleep in my arms. One time I met her on the street and she asked me if I was interested in her. I told her that I was but it wasn't really true. We went to bed but we didn't get round to doing much because we were expecting someone to come in. Eventually, I had sex with other girls but this was part of a group scene. We were in an apartment and I was feeling tired, so the man suggested I lay down for a while. I went into the bedroom and things began to happen. At first it was just the girl and myself and then the man joined us. Another time, with a different couple, I was more attracted to the man than the girl. She was very attractive but her attitude failed to excite me; she was too sexy in a 'Hollywood' sort of way. Somehow I didn't think that she was genuine'.

Curiosity is indeed often such a strong motivation that it can overcome quite deep-seated inhibitions. Those women who had not had sexual contact with members of their own sex frequently remarked that if the opportunity arose, they would probably accept because they 'wanted to see what it was like' or 'might learn something'. We have already seen that a turning-away from men due to an unpleasant experience may result in temporary homosexual relationship. Women, who for some reason have a fear of penetration, are often exclusively homosexual and it was interesting to note that some of the women in the study who were pregnant, and therefore more wary of penetration, either enjoyed masturbation more than they had done previously, or turned their sexual thoughts to love-making with women, where, of course, penetration was impossible: 'I have never given other women a thought', remarked one young mother, 'that is, until I was pregnant and I suddenly developed a strong desire to sleep with an old girlfriend of my husband. This desire was not fulfilled, but I think that I would enjoy sleeping with a woman in the same way I enjoy sleeping with a man'.

It is evident that homosexual attraction is neither rare nor to be excluded from the lives of heterosexual women. There were no signs that the heterosexual women who reported homosexual relationships did so with accompanying guilt feelings. The woman who condemned female homosexuality or reacted with horror to the thought of taking part in such activity herself was rare. To the average heterosexual woman, the thought of indulging in homosexual activities is not outrageous, neither from the point of view of possible enjoyment nor self-recrimination. Certainly the hysterical attitude which is common in the heterosexual male's attitude towards male homosexuality is not manifest in the case of women and lesbianism. Perhaps women have no need to cling so desperately to their feminine image as men. Motherhood or the supposed capacity for motherhood is sufficient evidence of femininity; there is no such easy route for men. Thus their sexual prowess with women has become their means of convincing both themselves and others of their maleness. In a culture which is obsessed with the idea that men should be men and women should be women, homosexuality among males has become synonymous with effeminacy.

I gained some insight into this problem during a fascinating interview with an American psychologist, Virginia Prince. Virginia began life as Charles. Charles was a transvestite with no homosexual leanings. After a traumatic divorce case when details of Charles' cross-dressing were splashed across newspapers, Charles became Virginia. 'I had nothing to lose so I decided to adopt the appearance and behaviour of a woman permanently and try to help others with similar problems to those I had experienced'. Virginia sees transvestism as a reaction against enforced maleness; she had invented a new word 'femophilia' — love of the feminine. She believes that the feminine side of the male personality is stolen from him during his upbringing when he is being prepared for his role as the aggressive male. Gender and sex she views as separate entities: 'You are born a certain sex, but gender is learnt'. Virginia claims that today men spend more time trying not to be women than they do trying to be men. She speaks ironically of the perfume which when prettily packaged and provided with a romantic name is sold to women, and when decanted into another bottle and given the name 'Russian Saddle – or some other ridiculous masculine image – will sell equally well to men under the guise of an after-shave lotion.

Her theory is that at present masculinity and femininity exist as two poles. She sees it as far easier for women to move towards the masculine pole than vice versa, thus a woman has room to express the masculine side of her nature whereas men suffer from greater restriction. This is the reason why there is less female than male homosexuality and why incidents of female transvestism are isolated.

I also feel that this explanation has relevance to the curious fact that female homosexuality is more socially acceptable than male homosexuality. Of course, female homosexuality has never been a punishable offence, thanks to the bigotted naivety of Queen Victoria – the wisdom of law means a lot to a great many people. But there are other reasons which contribute to a larger public acceptance of lesbianism, many of which may be eventually traced to Virginia Prince's hypothesis. The lesbian is less inclined to accentuate her homosexuality publicly by adopting masculine dress and habits. The 'camp' jargon and behaviour so often displayed as a defence mechanism by male homosexuals has no real parallel in the lesbian world. Even if a woman does adopt the short hair and tweed suit mode of dress she is still likely to be excused as she fits into either the role of the self-sufficient career woman who has been forced to veer towards masculinity to survive in the competitive male business world. Alternatively, the school-marm spinster in her brogues and floppy hat is considered more the eccentric of her community than as a sexual deviant and is regarded with benign amusement.

A lesbian is a woman and not a man – therefore in later life she may be more strongly drawn to a home and secure relationship. Lesbians embark on monogamous relationships with one another, more frequently and more successfully than male homosexuals. Because it is common for two women, widows, sisters, mother and daughter to live together as companions, they are not thought at all odd. Their relationship stands a better chance of survival than a similar relationship between two men because it is automatically accepted by the community and free from the strains of ostracism. In turn this liberates the lesbian from the necessity of short-term relationships and promiscuity which heterosexuals tend to find so distasteful in the male homosexual. In many cases one of the partners may have a child, the result of a failed heterosexual marriage, and this contributes further to the public eye's vision of respectability.

On a day to day level women are allowed to display openly a physical closeness which, especially in Great Britain, is not permissable for men. Women kissing one another farewell or walking arm in arm is never considered offensive. The sight of women demonstrating affection has somehow come to appear more aesthetic than two men doing the same and this follows through to love-making. A woman as an individual has more aesthetic appeal than a man. It was pointed out to me that recently a whole national exhibition of photography was devoted to the subject of women. 'There would never be such an exhibition with the male form as its subject', said my informant. She added, 'You know, apart from the occasional film star, I never hear women referring to men as beautiful, they are more appreciative of other women as aesthetic objects because that is the way in which our whole culture regards women'. Thus the image of two men making love can never contain the aesthetic value inherent within a similar image of two women. For a number of men, and indeed for some women, the fantasy of two women making love is full of erotic appeal. It is evident from literature that the lesbian fantasy is popular among men. Excitement comes from the thought that women whom they equate with passivity can be autonomously active in sex; here is sex for pure pleasure, totally divorced from the reproductive function.

Because there is less prejudice against female homosexuality in comparison to male homosexuality, it does not follow that there is no prejudice nor that a female homosexual does not suffer from the problems of self-acceptance I mentioned previously. Some women are more able than others to adjust to their homosexuality, but there is inevitably a struggle involved in the full acceptance of the implications of homosexuality. A woman who arrives at the conclusion that she is almost exclusively homosexual must also arrive at the realisation that for her life will be quite different to that of the majority of women. She will not marry, she will not have children, she will be forced to support herself financially for the rest of her life, she will probably have to make a secret of her sexual orientation as far as employers, workmates and certain social contacts are concerned, the selection of sexual partners is limited and the chances of finding a secure and loving relationship in which sex plays its part are far less than those of the heterosexual.

Laura first became aware of her lesbian tendencies when she was quite young although she says that at the time she was not aware of the full significance of them. True to the traditional image, she was a tomboy and always felt much more attracted towards girls than boys. She was thirteen when she embarked upon her first affair with a girl five years older than herself. She had taken up skating and met her girlfriend at the rink where she was a professional skater: 'One afternoon we were in the clubroom at the icerink and I was changing my boots. My bootlace got stuck and she came over to give me a hand. She managed to unknot the lace for me and, while I was leaning over, she just kissed me. It all seemed quite natural'.

Laura's parents were extremely wealthy. Her mother was a former silent filmstar, glamorous, petite, blonde and pretty. She was also an alcoholic. Laura's mother had been married three times and her father five times. Laura adored her father and when her parents were divorced she was forced to live with her mother as her father was in the Army because of the war.

She discovered her mother's alcoholism and from the age of twelve she spent a great deal of her time putting her drunk mother to bed and generally looking after her. She also remembers the following incident which took place when she was six: 'I woke up in the night and went in to Mama. I don't remember the details, but she was in bed with this rather gorgeous blonde showgirl. I found them in, shall we say, incriminating circumstances'. Laura believes that on the female side of her family homosexuality is hereditary. By the time she was sixteen Laura felt that she was definitely 'out of line'. 'I decided that there must be something in this sex lark and I had better find out about it. I freely admit that I tried but when it came down to it I just couldn't. Specifically there was this very attractive man; he was twenty-five and I was seventeen. We went off on a boat and things progressed as they usually do. I liked him tremendously as a person. I thought — well, if I was going to try and find out about sex I might as well go with somebody I liked. We got past the initial stages but when we got to the 'crunch', as the saying goes, I just couldn't go through with it. I felt physically sick, nauseous. I literally threw him halfway across the cabin. He was shocked and hurt and I apologised. He was upset because he thought that it was something he had done. I was really in a state'.

From then on Laura realised that her sexual orientation was homosexual. At one time she had a six-year relationship with another woman which was blighted by jealousy because the other woman was bi-sexual. She has achieved astonishing success in her career and appears to have sublimated the desire for children and a mate into her business. She gets on well with men and enjoys their company but feels no sexual desire for them whatsoever. She is ready for a permanently-based relationship with another woman but not to the extent that she would plunge into such a relationship indiscriminately.

She has found that married women will seek a lesbian partner through boredom. This boredom stems from two sources, boredom with their husbands as lovers and with empty afternoons after the housework is over. 'I would think that there are quite a large number of married women who have had lesbian relationships at some time or another. I have met quite a number who are having lesbian affairs despite their marriage. It is said of lesbianism that you can never break free of it and this is probably true. I know a woman who had a lesbian relationship before she got married and she was happily married for twelve years. She thought that it was all in the past. When she was forty-five she went to a party where she happened to see the other woman in the room and it was just like that — her marriage went completely on the rocks. She got divorced and went off to live with another woman. I think that if a woman has had lesbian experiences they will always crop up'.

Laura was appalled at the amount of ignorance which prevails concerning lesbian love-making and laughed at the general opinion that lesbians wield dildoes and strap artificial penises to themselves. 'It must be remembered that lesbians attach a great deal more importance to affection rather than just the actual physical side of sex. The sensuous touch of the body can sometimes be full of meaning. I have never met any lesbians who use artificial aids, such as dildoes. Any girl who wants another female doesn't want an imitation of a male. If they do, well let them go and get the real thing. It goes without saying that one woman knows another woman's body much better than a man and that she can work another woman up to a much higher state than a man can, simply because she possesses more control. As a woman you know exactly what will excite your partner. I once had an affair with a nymphomaniac. She was bi-sexual and loved sex. She told me that she had never had the same satisfaction from a man that she had had from me. Let's face it, a woman has a much greater control over a long period of time than a man and with someone as highly sexed as a nymphomaniac, this is important. Basically, I suppose lesbians are much more sensual than men — that is, the play on the body and the nerves of the body is much greater than in the heterosexual relationship. A number of women have complained to me that the men, once they have had their orgasm, couldn't be less interested and nine times out of ten the woman is left unsatisfied. I realise that this is elementary, but it's amazing the number of men who are concerned solely with their own satisfaction. What most men are not aware of is that women's backs are particularly sensitive. The nerve centres are very sensitive, much more than the breasts which many men make such a fetish of. You can work up a woman to a tremendous pitch by caressing the body, gently, sensitively. There are of course many variations of the theme — other areas which excite women are the back of the knees and the thighs. Also, behind the ears and neck. It depends on the individual, but I would say that the average woman needs forty-five minutes of love play before she reaches her peak'.

Although she was somewhat scornful of men, Laura enjoyed 'keeping up with them' in the business world. Her attitude was not so derogatory as that of Joan, now in her fifties and the 'widow' of a lesbian 'marriage'. With her short-cropped hair, incessant smoking, heavy clothes and swinging gait, she looked her part as a man hater. 'My father was a civil engineer and he was out working on the first project of the Assam Dam. I was only three months old when he died out there, so I never saw him. My mother married again when I was ten. I never liked my step-father. I resented him. He was in the Indian Civil service and he had to go out to India. My mother didn't really play fair with him and when it came to it, she wouldn't leave me. He went out there and drank himself practically stupid and had to come back here and retire. They were always rowing. Not long after they had been married my mother refused to have sex with him. They had separate rooms. One day he asked me if I would show him my breasts. I overheard my mother telling him that he must never lay a hand on me. I was very frightened and thought he was going to assault me. I would never be left alone in a room with him — I didn't like the way he looked at me. I was about fifteen when he asked me to show him my breasts.

'My mother always said never believe anything men tell you, they are dangerous animals. She never spoke about my real father to me. She put me against men right from early childhood. I have never considered men as worth anything. Even today, they take up such a patronising attitude to women. Sometimes I get on alright with them, but I have to talk to them on their own ground. I can't bear anything flirtatious. When I was a child I never bothered much with other friends, especially boys, although I always had boys' toys like tin soldiers and forts. I never wanted to play with dolls — I hated dolls. I suppose that I first became really aware of my lesbian inclinations through a senior girl at school. She came into the dormitory and got hold of me. I was about nine years old. I didn't know anything about sex then. I didn't really know what was going on. She said that I was cold and that she was going to cuddle me up. I thought it was a bit funny the way that she was behaving, but it didn't seem to impress me at all. It didn't carry on because I think that she got into trouble, although I was never spoken to about it.

'I was never told anything about sex. I heard other girls talking about it. When I was thirteen my mother came to me and told me about menstruation and I was horrified and thought that it wouldn't happen to me. I remember crying my eyes out. I didn't want to think that I was going to be the same as everybody else. When it did happen I kept it dark for as long as I could. I was terribly sensitive over it and most embarrassed in case anyone noticed that anything was wrong. The other girls at school would get themselves excused from games and gymnastics when they had their periods, but I would never admit to it. I was disgusted by it. I don't know why, but I have never liked babies and the way people speak about having children, it has always seemed distasteful to me. My mother made me feel rather guilty about sex, because she would never talk about it. She would never say anything at all risqué in front of me. She was very much obsessed with me. I couldn't have a letter without her wanting to know who it was from, and what was in it. She was always very possessive.

'I never went out with boys at all. I have never felt the need — it's just my make-up — I can't help it. I didn't have any kind of sexual experience, apart from the incident at school, until I was about twenty-three when I met a girl and started an affair. Her mother was dying of cancer and I was sympathetic and that's how it started. We went away on a holiday together. Eventually we lived together, then after five years, she got married. I was totally disgusted and very upset at the time as I had no idea that she was bi-sexual. I didn't realise for a long time that she was going out with a man.

'Later I met another girl who had been involved in a murder case. I felt very sorry for her and she came to London, changed her name and lived with my mother and myself. However, my mother didn't like her so she and I moved into a house across the road and lived alone. I was very much in love with her. She died four years ago from cancer. It has left a great void in my life — after all we were together from 1939 until her death. It was really like a marriage relationship, she was very domesticated and attended to all those things. We had a fairly regular sex life, but she wasn't really very keen. I didn't really mind this, although I once had a superficial affair with a married woman and felt very guilty. My friend found out and she was very upset. I still feel guilty about it. It's on my conscience. I think that it was always very difficult for other people to understand the relationship I had with my friend. I would never try to attempt to explain it to anybody. You see, I have never had any real feelings of respect for any man. I have always thought that they were boars and disgusting pigs! I have had them running after me. It repulses me if I think that a man wants me, I feel quite violent towards them.

'There are an awful lot of myths about lesbian relationships, people think that they have cupboards full of dildoes, but that's not at all true. I think that the contention is true that lesbian love-making is often more pleasurable for women because for many men love-making is quite brutal'.

Sex seemed to have played little part in Joan's life. Her hatred of men had led her to seek an affectionate relationship with a woman and now it was over she felt lonely. She admitted that at her age she was unlikely to find such a relationship again and appeared resigned to her loneliness, relieved by a few 'motherly' friendships with younger women.

The attitude of younger lesbians towards men seems markedly different to those of their elders. The following lengthy interview with Maggy, a twenty-year-old research assistant, highlights this point. Maggy and her friends, most of whom are lesbians, despise the 'butch' image. They are as interested in pretty clothes as any heterosexual girls, enjoy the company of men and may have sexual relationships with men. I reproduce Maggy's interview from beginning to end. Psychiatrists may say that her development was arrested at that stage where a girl has 'crushes' on her teacher or best friend and I must admit that I found it hard to accept that this attractive and remarkably intelligent young girl would not ultimately find herself in the position of mother and wife. In fact, if her hypothesis at the conclusion of the interview is ever realised, I see no reason why this should not happen.

'When I was about twelve years old, I had a "crush" on the headgirl of my grammar school although at the time I realised that it was something more than a crush. She was about six years older than me but we were very good friends. We used to go for walks together and I can distinctly remember one occasion when we sat down for a rest and I wanted her to touch me. It was about this time that I began to realise that I was attracted to girls rather than boys. I was bothered by the fact that my attraction was towards females and as I got older it worried me a great deal because I knew that I had to hide it. At school one usually went around with one's girlfriend outside of school, thus if it had become apparent it would have meant social ostracism. If ever the girls as school discussed lesbians it was always to say that they were sick. Sometimes I resented this, but usually I went along and laughed with them.

72

'I always went out with boys. I enjoyed their company very much. I still enjoy the company of men. I can't tolerate the attitude that many lesbians have towards men in thinking that they are inferior. After all, men form fifty per cent of the world and you can't just shut them out. But sexually my relationships with boys were dead. I could and can give any male a good lay simply because I can simulate response. No guy who has ever slept with me could ever complain and accuse me of being frigid because I can react as they want me to. I used to do this when I was a teenager. The first time I had sex was when I was seventeen. I got up afterwards and thought, "Oh hell, is this all it's about?" I wasn't even aware that he had entered me. I really don't know why I allowed it to happen because I wasn't at all excited. However, after that I had about four affairs with men. I suppose it was because if I go out with a girl I want to go to bed with her and in the same way I know that if a guy goes out with me, he wants to go to bed with me, so I comply. It means nothing to me but I can understand that it is important to them as it would be to me if I was straight.

'It wasn't long after I had lost my virginity that I had my first active lesbian affair. I went to a party where I met a girl whom I found immediately I could talk to. We began talking about drama and it was literally like smoking pot or something because we got high mentally through talk. Her boyfriend came into the room and tried to get in on our conversation but he couldn't. There was just her and me. It was the most incredible sensation, just like being in a bubble. Eventually I had to leave. I only knew this girl's first name and when I left we just shook hands. But she looked at me so intensely that I knew something was going to happen. I was really worried because I had felt something that I had never felt before, even though I had been attracted to a couple of my friends and had come into contact with a lesbian. Previously I had shied away from any lesbian relationship simply because I was scared.

'However, the following Monday at school, just as I was trying to figure out how I could contact this girl, another friend came up and said: "I believe you met S at the weekend. She has asked me for your phone number." I asked this other girl for S's surname and when I got home, I rang her. We talked for about an hour. It was quite incredible because everything I liked she liked. She said that she would ring again in the week and she did. By this time I was out of my mind. I was in love and this was it. Before this I had always been very hard and cynical and love was something which people wrote about but which never really happened.

'The first time that we went out was on a Saturday. I used to work and she met me before I began work at eight o'clock. We met for lunch and she invited me home for tea. We went up to her room and sat on the bed. We were talking about all the boys we had been out with and slept with and I remember having the experience of coming completely outside my body and watching the two of us talking. I was going mad. I was terrified that I wouldn't be able to control myself. Suddenly she asked me what I thought about her. I told her that I liked her very much and she put her hand inside mine and asked me if I was frightened. Of course I lied and said I wasn't. After that she kissed me and it was fantastic. She just said, "Oh, thank God that's over", and we went out. I was so relieved because I would never have dared start anything for fear of being rejected. We went and sat on the beach and talked. I was able to talk in a way that I had never been able to do before. I invited her to tea the next day. We went into my room and she lay down on my bed. She kept telling me to lie down next to her, but I couldn't bring myself to. It was all terribly dramatic. After tea we went out for a walk. I had an old broken-down beach hut. We went in there and made love. It was fantastic.

'This affair lasted for ten months. One New Year she was ill. We had promised to see the New Year in together but she made me go to a party which I didn't want to go to. However, I went along feeling really miserable and stayed the night. The next day there were a couple of guys there who were very nice. It was quite obvious that I was going to end up in bed with one of them. I tried to get out of it, but there was no way I could so I went to bed with him I knew that I had to tell S. I had no idea why I had gone to bed with this guy because I felt that I needed S more than I needed myself. I would have given her my life. When I told her she went crazy and nearly killed me. I had made vague arrangements to see this guy the following weekend. During the week S came to see me. She was extremely upset and crying. We were in my bedroom when my parents came in. They were showing someone around the house. They didn't say anything but as they left my father gave me the most strange look. The following Monday I was in bed when my mother came in and asked me if I had got any lesbian inclinations. I nearly fell out of bed with shock. Of course I denied it and she said no more.

'It turned out that when I met this boy, his friend's girl hadn't turned up so S was able to come with us to make up a foursome. About two months later, S and I were still going out with these two boys. We were having a sort of foursome. It was really hell for me and all rather weird. If we stayed at the boys' flat when they went off to work in the morning S would come into bed with me. It was something I didn't want to happen at all. It tore me apart. These boys asked us to go and stay with them for a weekend. I asked my mother if I could go and she told me to ask my father. I thought this was very strange because she usually made the decision herself. She told me that she didn't want me to go because she didn't want me to be with S whom she referred to as a bitch. Soon after she threatened to go to S's home which eventually she did. She had phoned up and said that she was going which gave S half an hour to tell her mother why. S's mother was fabulous about it all and told my mother that at least this way we couldn't get pregnant. After that S wasn't allowed to come to my place any more but they didn't prevent me from going there. This went on for four months until I was planning to leave school. I was to work as a bus conductress for the holiday break in a nearby town. S and I planned to move into digs together.

'One night just before I was due to leave I had returned from S when my mother said: "You've been with that cow again." She just slammed my dinner down and walked out. I finished my meal and went to find my mother to ask her what she meant. She turned round and told me that I was perverted so I spat at her. I had hysterics. I began crying and beating on the wall. My mother came tearing after me with my father. They yelled and screamed about how perverted it was and how I would be derided. It went on until I was a wreck. I was sitting at the top of the stairs and my father was halfway down just shouting abuse. All of a sudden he looked at my mother and said: "I wonder which she is, butch or fem." This was enough, I went for him. He threw me down the stairs and punched me in the stomach. This was the action of the civilised man who had brought me up to be a free-thinking intellectual!

'Eventually, I had to promise that S wouldn't come to my digs. I suppose that this incident should have made me think that I was really perverted but it didn't. I had previously weighed up the pros and cons. I knew it was something which had to be kept hidden from certain people simply because it would offend them. I came to the conclusion that if I expect people to be tolerant of me as a lesbian, then I have got to be tolerant of people being intolerant towards me. I accept the fact that I am in a minority and that to most people lesbianism is a perversion.

'The next day my parents told me that they had made an appointment for me with a Harley Street psychiatrist, so I just walked out. It didn't really bother me because I had never been particularly close to my parents. In fact until I fell in love with S, I was completely hard. The news of a death or something of that nature never ever moved me. My parents have never mentioned my lesbianism since then. In fact, they now think that I am straight.

'S telephoned my mother and told her that we wouldn't be seeing one another any more. Of course we did but then the time came for her to go away to a different college. Also, she had been going out with a boy because I wasn't always there and I had started feeling attracted to a lesbian woman who worked on the buses with me. Eventually this woman, J, asked me out. This put a strain on my relationship with S because she knew that it was alright for us both to go out with boys because we would always come back to one another, but where another woman was involved, things were rather different. I'm not really sure why I went ahead and went out with this woman. I think that I realised that S and I were coming to an end. I was terrified at the prospect of her going to college and finding someone else. We had had ten months of everything being at fever pitch, everything was an extreme. When any relationship burns at that peak for so long it has to burn out.

'J was 33. I knew that she was a lesbian. We went out for a drink. She hadn't realised that I was a lesbian so I told her. My relationship with this woman was totally different to that with S. We used to do the horses and the dogs and things like that. We were very happy because it wasn't an intense relationship. She had a wordly intelligence which attracted me. I think that lesbians almost always recognise one another. I'm not sure what it constitutes, but often I can look at a girl and know that she is a lesbian, even if she is not an active lesbian. J always said that it was in the eyes. I don't go around looking for it but I'm sure I can recognise lesbianism when I come across it. Something happens, there is a kind of emanation. I read somewhere that garbage is drawn to garbage — similar types attract each other; I suppose this is what happened between J and myself.

'When the time came for me to go to college I decided that I would have to try to be straight. I thought that being a lesbian was going to make life too difficult. This wasn't because I had suffered particularly from being a lesbian. When I worked on the buses, which was the first time that I had come into contact with a group of lesbians (all the women apart from two were homosexual), I found it was acceptable. This was because it was almost a community unto itself. However, when I arrived at college I thought that there couldn't possibly be any lesbianism there. I decided to calm down and wait for whatever happened. Oddly enough it turned out that I was very wrong. This is when I decided that homosexuality is not something which one finds in isolated corners of society. It's everywhere. At this time I knew full well I was a lesbian, but I suppose that I

76

was trying to escape from myself. It was while I was at college that I realised that I had to come to terms with it and that if I was going to be a lesbian I may as well be a happy lesbian.

'I produced a play while at college. There was a very attractive girl in the case, P. She started to talk to me one night and told me that she had had two relationships in her life, one physical and one emotional. She said that the emotional relationship had been with a girl. When I told her that I had had a couple of affairs with women, she announced that she thought she was in love with me. I could hardly believe it because although she had had an emotional relationship with a girl, it had never come to anything because she was straight. It was awful because I didn't know what to do. She was mixed up because she couldn't accept her own lesbianism and I was trying to fight my attraction to her. This went on for about two weeks and eventually we embarked on an affair which lasted until I left college. There were a number of complications in the relationship. To begin with there was another girl in my year who was engaged. Sometimes P and I would make up a foursome and go out drinking with her and her boyfriend. Then one night this girl declared that she was in love with me. It was a dreadful situation. She kept following me around college and it became embarrassing. At the same time I was getting involved with my French lecturer who was hung up because she said that she couldn't have an affair with me and teach me at the same time.

'One evening this girl was stuck in town and had to stay the night at my flat. Of course, that was it . . . we made love. P was dreadfully upset by this and I told this girl that she just had to go back to her boyfriend because I wasn't prepared to ruin her life. She went, but for two weeks after that I would come home to find her there crying her eyes out. She used to walk five miles to my house to see me. One evening the doorbell rang and there was this girl with her boyfriend. She had told him how she felt and he had brought her round to ask if she could stay with me for a month. He said: "Look, she wants you. I know she's going to marry me, but she wants you. A day isn't enough for her so let her stay and get it out of her system." I refused and finally, after a lot of talking, he took her away. By this time I was so confused about everything that I started drinking a lot. I got neuralgic headaches and used to go to college drunk. Finally, I couldn't stand it and went to a doctor who sent me to a psychiatrist.

'At this time I realised that when I was two and my younger sister was born, I was terribly jealous. Apparently I completely rejected my mother and from then on became a complete lone wolf. Even if I fell down I wouldn't let my mother make a fuss of me. I don't know whether or not this had anything to do with my becoming a lesbian. I am interested in psychology but I never felt that this psychiatrist helped me much. Eventually I managed to sort myself out and moved up to London with a friend and together we got into London's lesbian scene. We joined a well-known lesbian club and I found that I got on very well. Most of my close friends are lesbians but at the same time I have been going out with a man from work who doesn't know I'm lesbian. He is the most considerate man I have ever met and I allow him to make love to me. I can't ever have an orgasm when he is making love to me unless he makes love like a woman. The rest of the time I simulate an orgasm. I can think about anything while I am making love to him and my body just makes mechanical motions. I do it because I want to please him.

'For me sex is a combination of mental and physical attraction. When I go to the lesbian club I can't just go with anyone. What I most dislike about the lesbian set up is the "butch—fem" scene. I think that perhaps I am predominantly butch, but it doesn't really make any difference to me, what attracts me is the person. If I make love to a woman, afterwards I want to be made love to, that's when I have an orgasm. The fact that a man has to have an ejaculation has a lot to do with the way that he makes love. With a woman she can control the situation exactly and for as long as is necessary. A woman making love to another woman is just as instinctive as a man making love to a woman. It isn't something you have to learn. Few lesbians use dildoes. This is a myth. My opinion is that if a woman wants to use a dildo, she may as well go with a man and have the real thing.

'Sex is very important to me and I have had a very happy sexual relationship with most of the people I have been with. It is really quite fantastic. Having an orgasm is always in colours and shapes. It's like a black glove, a smooth shape. I got outside myself into this shape. The two of us are completely joined, there is no separate entity. It's like a skinless balloon. I think that I am truly a lesbian but I might be able to get married. I suppose I consider it because most girls do at some time. What will probably happen is that I will settle down with another woman. I wouldn't bother about the ostracism because I find that the sort of people I want as friends are those who are tolerant. I think that there is more tolerance towards male homosexuality than lesbianism. People have accepted that men make love to one another, or if they haven't accepted it, they are at least aware of it. I am sure there are some people who still won't accept the fact that women should want to make love to one another.

'Any woman is capable of having a lesbian affair. They might meet a woman whom they love and it doesn't matter to them whether she is a man or a woman, simply that she is. I would never go out of my way to initiate an affair with a woman I knew to be straight. It would probably unleash too much suffering because of the guilt she would feel. I am sure that the sort of "marital" relationship which can exist between a man and a woman can also exist between two women. Women want to settle down and if two women take out a lease then that can be as binding for them as a marriage contract. I often think that two women can be closer than a man and a woman because of this thing about a woman being aware of what another woman wants. She had this insight simply because she is the same sex. There are disadvantages insomuch as it is so much easier for lesbians to be promiscuous. It is so easy because there is no danger of pregnancy. Also, lesbians tend to age less easily. They have to keep themselves young because there is so much competition. If a woman marries, then her husband is there — he's been caught. But in the lesbian world there is no real marriage and always someone ready to step in your place.

'I certainly think that people are not so hung up about lesbianism as they were. Among young people it doesn't matter what sort of sexual orientation a person might have. Young lesbians are far less guilty than the older ones, which is why they despise the masculine-type suits and butch image. The sex-difference gap is closing and people are now being more accepted as people rather than men or women. One hopes that the whole label system of "heterosexual", "homosexual", and "bi-sexual" will just disappear and people will just be people'.

It is safe to say both from this study and from examining sources that the great majority of women like their sex straight. Heterosexual deviation is extremely rare among women; it may manifest itself in the female's fantasy world but it is infrequently a necessary part of sexual fulfilment in the world of reality. Fetishism, cross-dressing, and overt sexual sado-masochism belong almost exclusively to the erotic terrain of the male. If women do adopt rubber garments or brandish the whip it is usually in order to satisfy their partner and their own excitment is a product of the excitement they are causing their partner. A woman feels sexually aroused when she knows that she is arousing a man; this is why women claim that they 'feel sexier' in 'naughty' underwear. It is not the underwear alone it is the knowledge of what it can do!

Many marriages fail because wives find it difficult to comply with their husband's fetish. Certainly it is not easy for a woman to understand fetishism because it is so outside her own experience but, as I have said, luckily it is possible for a man to transmit his excitement to the woman and loving wives often give in to their husband's fetish simply because they are aware of the pleasure it gives him. I agree with Colin Wilson who suggests in his book, *The Origins of the Sex Impulse* (London, 1963), that women are less open to deviation because their attitude to sex is far more romantic and emotionally motivated than men who are closer to the physical and plainly erotic aspects of sexuality.

Undoubtedly, women can come in for the raw end of the deal where deviation or perversion is concerned. One woman I interviewed couldn't seem to escape from men who made rather exceptional demands of her. 'For some reason' she said, 'most of the men to whom I appeal are perverts. I have been chased by men with a thing about rubber macs and by those who wanted me to trample on them while I was wearing high-heeled shoes. I have had four affairs with men like that'. The woman concerned is now forty-five, a former professional dancer, and her mannerisms and appearance are still charmingly 'theatrical'. She is at present involved in her third marriage. She was educated at a convent school and, after the death of her father, ran away to begin her stage career.

'When I was sixteen and appearing in a show, I met my first husband. He came to the stage door and asked to take me out. He was an extremely handsome man with a vital personality and I was completely captivated by him. Within four days he had bought a special licence. I forged my age and we were married. I married him for a number of reasons. Firstly, because he was so handsome and charming; and secondly, because he lived in Paris and I loved the idea of living there. I thought that if I wrote from Paris and told my mother that I had got married, she would have to accept the fact, and that would clear up my family problems. To an extent this turned out to be true. We got married and flew over to Paris. I was still incredibly naive and when we were preparing for bed, I felt nervous and excited. My husband went into the bedroom and I got into bed. I was waiting for him when he walked in. I have never been so shocked. He was dressed as a woman with gold earrings in his nipples. I just burst into tears. After the initial shock was over he told me that he couldn't have intercourse but all the same he began to make love to me. He kissed my genitals and this gave me such a thrill that I came to orgasm. I nearly hit the ceiling. He had an orgasm too.

'Next day I thought about all this and decided that it was horrible, but I knew that if I went home my mother wouldn't have me back. So I had to stay. My husband and I went on like this for about a year. I still had my virginity. However, I was getting orgasms out of this kind of sex and he seemed to enjoy it, so I didn't feel too bad. Apart from this, he was a wonderful man and very fond of me. He had a marvellous personality and we used to get on very well. He said that he had never actually had intercourse, in fact he couldn't, but he was nevertheless attracted to women and wanted to be married. After a while we decided that we wanted children. We went to a clinic but there the doctors discovered that my husband was infertile. This and his being a transvestite were both so strange because he was an athletic type and played all sorts of sports. He was a big virile-looking man. After we had been to the clinic he got it into his head that I should go out and bring home a man to make love to me while he (my husband) was tied up in the bathroom watching through the glass door. I didn't like the idea, but I was so fond of him that I agreed. He waited three nights tied up in the bathroom, until I eventually picked up a man in a bar and brought him home. This man knew nothing of my husband. Anyway the whole thing went off as planned. This man made love to me and I lost my virginity. I didn't enjoy it because it was messy and it hurt. I didn't have an orgasm. Afterwards I vomited. I felt that I would never have an orgasm with anyone other than my husband. I really didn't want to repeat this performance, but my husband insisted. He said that every time it had to be with a different man, because he didn't want me to form an attachment to anyone else. He said that he got a tremendous kick out of watching us while he was tied up. He said that he felt that he wanted to rush out and save me; but of course, being tied up prevented him from doing so.

'It was then that I met this Jewish boy. He was about my age and I liked him very much. Eventually, we made love. It was marvellous. He kissed my genitals and, as with my husband, this gave me intense orgasms. I also had orgasms during intercourse but they weren't the same. They were less exciting. I think that I had come to associate intense orgasms with oral stimulation of the genitals. Our affair went on for about eight months and then my husband found out. He couldn't take my infidelity in this way and our marriage broke up. I returned to England and my lover followed me. All was well for a while and then he had a heart attack and died.

'After this, my husband came looking for me and we went back together. However, this time he was worse. He made me sew his testicles together with needle and thread. This petrified me because there was so much blood and I thought that he was going to die. He found an old prostitute and he wanted me to go to her. The idea was for this old bag to be the mistress. She was to give me orders and then I was to give my husband orders. This was the end for me, and I left him again.

'One of my affairs lasted for quite some time. He was a Cabinet Minister and rather similar to my husband. He did all the things my husband used to, plus some very filthy things. He expected me to urinate on him and things like that. However, he was different inasmuch as he always finished up having normal intercourse. I suffered all his perversions because I suppose that I was in love with him. He had made for himself a special maid's uniform which he would wear. He wanted to be my slave. He didn't look as grotesque as my husband when he dressed up in women's clothes, because he was a smaller man and really quite dainty. As with my ex-husband, I didn't get anything sexually out of his performances. I got my thrill from cunnilingus and subsequent intercourse. I didn't enjoy the odd things. I found that my orgasms were different with different people. With my first husband I would have several. My body would feel as if it were breaking apart and I would make a terrible noise. I didn't have to try for it and, when it came, it sent me to fever pitch. With the Jewish boy, I would have similar feelings with the first orgasm, which came through cunnilingus. But the orgasm which came through intercourse wasn't the same. It was good, but I had to work for it. It didn't send me to extremes. With the Cabinet Minister, I used him to my own ends, I had to suffer his parade so I would make him do things for me, like kissing my genitals to give me these intense orgasms. Again, these were most intense and those brought about through intercourse were nice, but I felt that I could have done without them.

'After the Minister, I had a boyfriend who was a drinker and drink influenced my sex life. Just before love-making, he would give me some amyl nitrate and take some himself. It didn't do anything for me. In fact, I found the smell rather disturbing. He took a long time to come to orgasm and I found that because of the drink, I was the same. I had one orgasm with him but I didn't enjoy it madly, so I put an end to our affair.

'Then I met my second husband. He was a virile, good-looking Irishman who thought that everything but ordinary intercourse was revolting. He was a rough man and wanted to satisfy himself. He couldn't have cared less about satisfying me. Of course, after what I had been used to, I couldn't understand this plain bashing away. I didn't have an orgasm with him. We didn't have sex before we were married and that was a mistake. Sex for me became a punishment. Because of this, I went to see a doctor, as a result of which I had an operation which gave me a plastic enlargement to my vagina. I was terrified of becoming pregnant, because I didn't think that he was the sort of man who should be a father. He used coitus interruptus. He was a Roman Catholic and wouldn't use condoms,

82

so after my operation I used a cap. However, nothing seemed to solve the problem. One night he became so violent that I called the police and left him. Unfortunately, when I arrived back in London I found that I was pregnant. I thought that perhaps a child would make a difference to our marriage, so when he came looking for me I went back to him. He thought it was great because he could have sex every night without having to worry about coitus interruptus. By the time that the baby was born I had had enough of him. I never had orgasms when we had sex and I was terribly frustated, so I left him again.

'I engaged a nanny and went to work in a club. I met a man who wanted to live with me so I soon gave it up. I was in love with this man and we had a marvellous two years together. Our sex life was a great success. He was "normal". We would spend time on love play and then have intercourse. I always had orgasms. It was all rather fabulous. Then his wife, from whom he was separated, started to kick up a fuss. He had to give her money and he couldn't afford me as well. Also, his family started to interfere, and the whole thing blew up.

'I was terribly unhappy. The day after we had spent our last night together, I went drinking at a friend's club. He suggested that four of us including his girlfriend plus a man I had just met, should go back to my place to carry on drinking, so we did. When dawn came, we were all tired. George, the stranger, couldn't get back to his home so I said that he could stay. We were so high that I thought that we would simply go to sleep. But he made love to me and it was marvellous. I enjoyed every minute. We had an affair and I thought: "If I marry this one, perhaps it will be the answer". For the first six months, things couldn't have been better. I educated him in cunnilingus and our sex life was perfect. But his money came to an end and we couldn't go out and enjoy ourselves. Gradually, he made me cut down on my friends.

'Now, when he comes home from work, all he does is sit and watch telly and then falls asleep. He drops hints early in the evening if we are to have sex later. I hate this because I like it to be spontaneous. I have no desire for him now. I am alright once we get into bed and I get started; then I enjoy myself. But I suspect that it can't last much longer. I still do have orgasms. I would leave him immediately if I didn't'.

This is a fantastic story and quite rare. Few women have found themselves on the receiving end of quite such extraordinary male deviations.

One of the most common deviations, in fact it is almost too common to be considered any longer a deviation, is the 'spanking phenomenon' —

erotic arousal through spanking on the buttocks. Although few women in the survey had experienced this, correspondence such as that in the columns of *Penthouse* and *Forum* magazines have proved that it is not at all unusual. Those women in the survey who had experienced 'spanking' seemed to enjoy receiving rather than doing the spanking: 'I have now found that the only way I am stimulated to orgasm is through being spanked', said a twenty-year-old single girl. 'My fiancé and I begin with a lot of conventional love play and then when we are both ready, he flicks me over his knee and gives me a good spanking with his hands. After resting for a few moments in one another's arms we have intercourse during which I have very intense orgasm'.

The thought of being spanked appears as amusing rather than exciting to most women and it certainly should not be confused with true sado-masochism which involves far more complex and painful manoeuvres than simple spanking. It is not difficult to understand why some women might be aroused, through being spanked. The buttocks are an erogenous zone, more so in some than in others and this factor combines with the psychologically erotic stimulation of the 'dominating' male.

One woman who was worried about her enjoyment of spanking was reassured by her doctor that she was not a masochist but anal-erotic: 'I am unfailingly stimulated by standing beside my partner or in his arms while he strokes my back and buttocks. I am almost too sensitive between the buttocks — a phenomenon that certain shrewd and devious young men have not failed to discover. Sometimes this has led to activities I had not even thought possible and which would be considered by society as beyond the pale. With one of two men I have played my "little girl in the copse" fantasy. With a good "actor" my excitement mounts as soon as he says "take your knickers down I shall spank you". Obviously a person as gullible as myself is bound to come in for some trouble and I suppose that I am lucky that this little fad has not caused me some serious harm. Once I take a lover, I try to refuse him nothing, so that the price of experiencing bliss is often no more than a burning bottom. Someone birched me, but I wouldn't like it again . . . Although I can't deny the pleasure I derive from being spanked by a man, to be hurt in any other way, or on any other part of the anatomy would leave me cold'.

The 'little girl in the copse' fantasy was explained: 'When I was about eight years old a total stranger accosted me in the copse behind our house. He said something about my trespassing and treated me to a hearty spanking. I dashed home and shut myself away, shocked and excited. I told no one. Days later I ventured back into the copse but found nobody.

I began to play a strange game in the copse, the sort I might play in my bedroom, imagining the stranger as some god, or perhaps a father figure. Then I met him again, and again he led me to a quiet spot where he turned me over his knee. This time to facilitate matters he took my knickers down. This made me feel I could never face a man again, but, of course, I faced him again. We met a score of times or so, often in an old hut in the copse. Each time I shyly accepted the spanking. One day he sexually assaulted me and I ran off, never to see him again'.

The acting out of such fantasies plays a greater part in the sex lives of both men and women than most care to admit and the fantasies which could be employed to accompany spanking, that is slightly masochistic fantasies, are pertinent to the whole subject of female sexuality as we will note in the following chapter.

6 Masturbation

A rigid morality, as many of the interviews have illustrated, can create considerable anxiety for those who are unable to conform or are constrained to repress their 'unacceptable' drives. The origins of such values have much of their roots in the Puritan ethic and its subsequent influence on the morality of the Victorians. Current attitudes to masturbation are more clearly understood, although not excused, if we look at them in relation to the background of Victorian beliefs and some of their barbaric practices. This following description should explain some of the lingering disapproval of masturbation and certainly indicates the harmful effect of such beliefs.

In his book *The Anxiety Makers* (London, 1969), Dr. Alex Comfort records the medical literature of the Victorians dealing with onanism which makes far more horrifying reading than some of the malpractices of the Marquis de Sade. Some of the preventive techniques used are reminiscent of medieval torture practice. Electric alarms were attached to small boys' penises at night so than any interferences would immediately arouse the parents. All manner of straps and harnesses were invented to prevent youngsters from touching their genitals and also every affliction under the sun was said to be the result of masturbation. Medical maniacs even went so far as to *invent* a disease, 'Spermatorrhoea', which they claimed was caused by masturbation. This bogus disease was supposed to weaken the intellect, disfigure the features and generally reduce the strength of the body.

There is little doubt that of all forms of sexual behaviour masturbation is probably the activity which has provoked the most hysteria, and which, even in these supposedly more enlightened times, is still attached to all kinds of ridiculous superstition and mumbo-jumbo.

It is now accepted that the number of children who do masturbate is far greater than those who do not. For some years now doctors have warned parents of the foolishness of making remarks such as 'don't let me ever catch you playing with yourself again', to children caught in the act, but then parents are assured that little Johnny or little Susie will soon quite naturally 'grow out of it'.

We now have the situation where it is acceptable and natural for children to masturbate and it is to be expected occasionally of adolescents as well. Certainly this has been something of a breakthrough from the evil ways of the Victorians but it is hardly a satisfactory attitude.

Despite the fact that most people masturbate — American studies set the statistics at ninety per cent of the male population and between seventy-five and eighty per cent of the female population — most people also feel that it is something which isn't quite right for adults. This may well be because, unlike masturbation in a child which is completely sensual and a game which makes them feel nice, masturbation in an adult is rooted in the psyche and in the main accompanied by fantasy of some kind or another. As far as the Roman Catholic church is concerned it is considered a sin and cannot be justified.

Yet the figures stand and neurosis continues. One criterion used in making judgements about masturbation is to consider it in terms of restraint and excess. The problem of defining the word 'excess' then arises. Where does excess begin? Where does one draw the line? Usually there is an extreme which will at least stand as fact and, in the case of masturbation, it is safe to say that where pain and inflammation of the genitals is caused then masturbation is excessive. Another useful contention is contained in the concept 'obsession'. Any behaviour which becomes *obsessive,* be it cleaning one's shoes or masturbating, may well be a symptom of psychosis. It is possible that a person not suffering from mental illness will masturbate during a period of intense stress or worry.

Boredom and feelings of inadequacy and lack of self-achievement may also result in compulsive masturbation, as in the case of this young housewife: 'I first remember masturbating at about the age of six or seven. I had a ring and I used to put it in between my legs and play with it. Eventually, I went on to use instruments such as a hairbrush handle which I would insert into my vagina. I now find that sometimes when I am reading something very erotic I can make myself come without even touching myself.

'Now that I am married I masturbate more than ever, almost every day. In the afternoon I get depressed because the children are asleep. I have nothing to do. Sometimes I will pick up a book and read about tortures or something similar. That way I can have an orgasm without moving. Reading about female torture stimulates me most which may have something to do with my having been raped when a teenager. I bought a book about rape and had three orgasms while reading it. I don't have an orgasm every time my husband and I have intercourse and yet I can make myself have as orgasm through reading almost any time I choose. I almost always masturbate this way because somehow I don't think it is as bad as using an implement'.

In this case as in similar cases, masturbation is a *symptom* and not a cause of the woman's boredom and depression. She is also quite unusual in the fact that she can bring herself to orgasm without digital stimulation.

Women can use various methods of masturbation but most involve some kind of caressing or pressure. There are women who masturbate to orgasm through manipulating their breasts, but it is more common for women to employ clitoral stimulation. Penis substitutes are not always necessary but they are used for psychological effect. Almost any available roughly phallic-shaped object is used, such as hairbrush handles. Various studies have also reported that not an uncommon method is to lie in the bath with the tap water running over the clitoris and pubic area.

In Japan, the gismo or dildo, is sold openly in shops and such instruments are part of the ancient Japanese cultural heritage. There is even the story of one Japanese empress who died through an infection caught through a radish she was using as a dildo, which became lodged in her vagina.

Certainly, even the Western woman may choose any implement for masturbation with great care. The implement is to her as much a comforter as the dummy is to a baby. She will no doubt develop quite a fondness for the object, which may be chosen through trial and error as in the case of this housewife whose husband was absent from home: 'I didn't have an orgasm until two years after my marriage and didn't masturbate before then. It began when my husband was in hospital for three months. I cuddled the pillow but that was not enough. I tried the handle of a spoon, a hairbrush — and then success — one of those little rose vases with a bulb at the end. Later I decided this was dangerous as it might break, so I used a small pestle bought for the purpose'.

In some South Pacific cultures baby boys and girls are taught to masturbate but in our own culture discovering masturbation is likely to be accidental, especially in the case of girls. One eighteen-year-old said that although she had seen another girl masturbate under her bedclothes and had been told that the girl was 'playing with herself', she still had no idea what it actually entailed. 'I still wouldn't know how to go about it', she said. Boys are more likely to discover masturbation through unexpectedly having an erection. In the case of girls it is early sexual arousal which is most likely to lead to masturbation and this frequently occurs around puberty: 'Just before I was in my teens I used to indulge in daydreams by the hour about romantic encounters with my favourite film stars. I wasn't sure what we would do together but my thoughts would so excite me that I would shut myself away and masturbate. I didn't have an orgasm on these occasions, although I would probably masturbate three or four times a week. I didn't have an orgasm until I was about seventeen. It happened by accident and I didn't know what had struck me. It seemed that the room darkened and something hit the top of my head. It's never been quite so dramatic since'.

The hormonal changes which take place in the body during puberty and adolescence and the resultant sexual tension may cause frequent masturbation. Also at these times sexual arousal occurs through petting and kissing without being followed through to intercourse. The young person is left high and dry and masturbation is the only outlet. The fact that a young person can masturbate may save them from many hurried and unsavoury sexual experiences. As one woman put it: 'During my teens I thought that it was better to masturbate than to give in to boys on casual dates'. However, in some the guilt association has bred such an aversion to masturbation that although their need is overwhelming, they cannot take action. 'I have never masturbated', said a highly-sexed nine-teen-year-old. 'I have felt the desire to do so but I have always stopped myself because the thought of doing it to myself put me off. At the time I always feel a great need for orgasm, but I just can't bring myself to do it'. But rather a woman should not masturbate at all than that she should masturbate but allow her guilt to suppress orgasm. Although I did not encounter such cases during this study there are many known incidents of women who have frequently masturbated, stopping short of orgasm. They feel that by suppressing orgasm the act of masturbation is less 'shameful'. If they knew the physical harm they were causing themselves these women would perhaps think again.

W.H. Masters and V.A. Johnson, during their laboratory research, found that during sexual excitation the uterus and walls of the vagina became engorged and showed swelling which is caused by fluids seeping into the tissue from engorged blood vessels. In some instances the uterus may enlarge to twice its normal size, and this was found to be more pronounced in women who had had one or more babies. The women who had not had babies lost all signs of engorgement ten minutes after orgasm, for those who had had children the resolution phase took up to twenty minutes. But in women who did not experience orgasm the uterus remained detectably engorged for as long as half an hour or an hour. The results of this research confirmed the gyneacological theory that a condition called chronic pelvic congestion, to which a number of gyneacological complications are related, could be traced in some cases to repeated year-by-year sexual arousal in a woman without orgasm.

But not only is the repeated suppression of orgasm in masturbation foolish from a physiological point of view, it may well also have marked psychological dangers. A young girl who has constantly suppressed orgasm in this way is likely to develop severe orgasm-anxiety and will find it difficult to experience orgasm when the time comes for a heterosexual relationship.

Some psychiastrists feel that the ability of a woman to masturbate to orgasm means that she has fully accepted her 'sexual self'. Those women who feel that their genitals are for the use of a man and not for their own pleasure often find it impossible to discover any meaning in love-making apart from the pleasure of having performed their duty; this is a masochistic attitude and far removed from the real meaning of sex as a shared experience.

For the sexually inexperienced woman, masturbation is a means of discovering the techniques which may be employed to ensure her satisfaction. She can then guide her partner and bring him to a better understanding of her sexual needs. It is far better that masturbation should be used in such a way as to ensure success in heterosexual love-making than as a release when love-making leaves the woman unsatisfied. No one can blame a woman for seeking to relieve her tension in this way but it is sad that she may have to do so. It does not take much imagination to realise why American statistics show that more married women than married men masturbate.

'Until I was married I don't think that I knew what a clitoris was', said a divorcee whose husband had never satisfied her sexually. 'I'd made vague attempts at masturbating when I was at school without any success whatsoever. Then one night my husband was asleep and I brought myself to a totally unexpected climax. From then on there was no looking back. Often when my husband left me frustrated I found myself searching for some kind of relief. Each time I masturbated I felt a tremendous guilt, as though I were an adultress and this became an obsession with me for some time. I shudder to think how frequently it took place. I had nothing to do and all day to do it in. I suggested to my doctor that I might be a nymphomaniac at which he hooted in derision. Yet twice a day is claimed to be excessive for a schoolboy! During my first year with my husband I masturbated on average something like four times a day. I admit that I still do it when necessary for I now live alone and sometimes I am without sex for weeks at a time'.

The married woman whose husband spends a considerable time away from home will use masturbation as an outlet. 'When my husband is away attending university I do masturbate. It is usually provoked by an external stimulus such as a letter from my husband which causes me to remember and hunger. I get about three letters a week. The orgasm I attain through masturbation is not of the same quality as that which I obtain during intercourse'.

The last remark was repeated by many women and the comparison between masturbation and love-making is made here by a young house-wife: 'The first time I masturbated was when I was eight months pregnant. I had never masturbated before this, although I can't really say why I hadn't done it previously. It certainly wasn't because I thought it was wrong. I just didn't have any desire to do so. I have masturbated alone many times since this first occasion but I don't really enjoy it. It seems so lonely and such a waste. It is nothing compared to the joys of sharing sex. I do tell my husband if I have masturbated during the day and this does seem to excite him. Conversely I can be aroused through thoughts of him masturbating. However, this doesn't occur often as we would rather share sex'.

Age seems to have little to do with whether or not a woman mastur-bates. The following quote is from an interview with a sixty-year-old widow who does have sex regularly with a lover. She too makes the point that masturbation is a lonely experience: 'I have masturbated from earliest memory. How it began is really shrouded in the past. Sometimes I can go for months without masturbating. I use it as a form of escape when I want to get out of this world and away from thoughts I have whenever something nasty upsets me. The whole point is for me to achieve orgasm. It's the one time that I can be certain of satisfaction, although orgasms brought about through masturbation are not as intense as those experienced during love-making. Unfortunately, when it is finished I realise that it wasn't what I really wanted, but before I reach orgasm it is something I feel that I need'.

'It is rather limiting', said a thirty-four-year-old single woman. 'I really do think that masturbating can make a woman rely on clitoral stimulation in order to have an orgasm, whereas with a good partner there are so many ways of doing so. Secondly I feel that it is bad psychologically, as there is always the feeling that there is 'someone missing'. I found that although it relieved physical tensions, mental tension remained which was due to the lack of closeness to another person'.

Certainly the benefit a woman may gain from masturbation, which has been known to relieve irritation, backache, pelvic discomfort and real pain, may be offset by emphasising feelings of loneliness. D.H. Lawrence, in an essay condemning masturbation, crystalised this when he said: 'There is no reciprocity. There is merely the spending away of a certain force, and no return', something a sensitive, and especially a lonely, woman will undoubtedly sense.

No doubt this is the underlying reason why masturbation is mostly accompanied by fantasy. 'I can only do it', said one woman, 'if I think of someone for whom I hold affection. Half the pleasure of intercourse comes from pleasing another person, so I have to imagine that I am doing just that'.

Sexual fantasies may begin at quite an early age although in children it is unlikely that they are aware that their fantasies are sexual. Those approaching puberty will probably have fantasies about film stars, television personalities or the teenage boy next door. In the main such fantasies will consist of kissing, hugging and the receiving of compliments. It is later, with the sudden burst of sexual feeling which accompanies adolescence, that the fantasies may become overtly sexual and the young person may suffer agonies at the knowledge that he or she is capable of 'such thoughts'. During this period boys, especially those who have no idea of what the unclothed female body might really be like, will indulge in all kinds of imaginings, projecting mental images of women in various states of undress. They will probably seek out magazines showing photographs of nudes to embellish their fantasy world. Girls on the other hand are unlikely to abandon the romantic elements of sex and their fantasies are thus more subtle than simple pictures of nude male bodies.

It is frequently the escape into a fantasy situation, then, which provokes masturbation. Except where tension is at a peak and the mere touching of the genitals can set off orgasm, masturbation is usually accompanied by fantasies. It is absolutely impossible to generalise as far as fantasies are concerned; each woman will have her own fantasies which will be dictated by the sort of person she is and her past sexual experience. For instance, two women reported that they fantasise that they are strip-tease dancers, or models for nude photographs. One felt that the reason for this was because she had small breasts and envied girls with large breasts – strip-tease dancers, etc. rarely have small breasts. The other woman said that it was because she wished that she was as uninhibited as is necessary for such work. Various lesbian fantasies cropped up and the reasons behind them varied from latent homosexuality to what was described as 'curiosity appeal'. One married woman in her twenties was best able to explain her feelings about her own attitude to sex by describing her fantasies: 'I fantasise that I am a prostitute. I imagine that a queue of men are waiting outside to make love to me. I also imagine that I am making love to my husband and a circle of men are sitting around watching. At the peak of excitement they take out their penises and masturbate. My most common fantasy is that people are watching me make love to my husband. I think this is because secretly I have always wished that I didn't care so much what people thought of me. I have wished that I could have been more daring and not prevented myself from having sex with boys because they might talk about me afterwards. I would like to have the kind of personality which would enable me to live for myself without giving a damn what other people thought'.

It is definitely possible for both men and women to learn about themselves by examining their reactions to their own masturbatory habits and fantasies. It is pointless believing that one is being liberal by 'tolerating' masturbation only in the young. The fact is that at some time or another, and to varying degrees, all men and women feel the urge to masturbate – better they they should come to terms with the urge, understand it and learn from it, than repress it.

7 Some Concluding Remarks

The present is certainly a bewildering time for a woman. In all likelihood she will have experienced an upbringing geared towards discouraging her sexuality yet, in adolescence, she will have encountered a barrage of advertising and other mass media which demands that her image and outward appearance should be as 'sexy' as possible.

Advertisements depicting sinewy, half-clad dollies, legs astride the phallic car, cigar, lollypop or whatever; the Lolita-age nymph screwing her naive young way round the cinema circuits; even the 'quality' Sunday columnist, luring her readers into the latest see-through couture – all set the scene. 'It's not enough just to look feminine any more', commented a young graduate, 'you've got to look like a siren'.

The point is that the newly promoted image of women as erotic hand-maidens, which was created as a reaction against Puritanism's mother-image, is as much a false extreme. But nevertheless it is not without effect and we are now faced with the ironic situation wherein many women are beginning to feel guilty because they think that they do not manifest *sufficient* sexuality. 'How about one of those, dear? – a husband might remark pointing to a colour supplement splash of a sensual negress garbed only in a necklace. The wife cringes, she knows he knows she has not got fifty guineas to spare from the housekeeping for such a piece of foolery, let alone the courage to wear it. She may joke a reply, but the barb will no doubt have found its mark.

'It is not by increasing her worth as a human being that she (woman) will gain value in men's eye, it is rather by modelling herself on their dreams', says Simone de Beauvoir. And although they claim to be struggling for equality both in and out of bed most women pay court to this unfortunate truth.

Wisely used the introduction of the contraceptive pill could herald a complete revolution in the female role concept. Unhindered by pregnancies and released to enjoy sex without worry women should now be able to develop to the full their 'human worth'.

'As a woman', said one young interviewee, 'I feel that I have a lot more to offer than the facilities of my womb for the procreation of the species. However, there does seem to be this deeply rooted need for children within most women. The thing is to ensure that motherhood becomes part of the general human experience and not an end in itself'. I think she is right. Nature is such that women will always have this need and the Pill certainly is not going to remove it, but it should help women to view motherhood as something of their own choosing rather than an imposed and inevitable occurence, and leave her with the knowledge that there are other alternatives. If men are to live in harmony with this 'new' woman – a woman who is educated, economically independent and sexually free in the sense that she is no longer limited by fear of pregnancy – then he must understand her. At the moment we are in the transition phase. The old taboos and traditions are still strong even if they are finding a different mode of expression. Great is the gap between liberation and permissiveness. Permissiveness implies allowance and condonement, and permission can only be a valid concept if authority prevails. Liberation is the freedom to behave naturally and unselfconsciously.

Resentment between the sexes, especially women resenting men, is more rife than ever. In the most sensitive area, concerning sex, women being interviewed often expressed this. 'I really do think that men are basically insensitive to women', remarked a twenty-three-year-old girl from New Zealand. 'The men I have known have not only been ignorant about the make-up of the female personality, but also about love-making itself. For them sex is purely physical and they don't become emotionally involved. I think that their orgasms are purely physical. Men use women all the time. One thing which really annoys me is their double standard: they think that they can get away with infidelity, while their wives and girlfriends must remain faithful. They resent it when their women become possessive. I think that women are basically monogamous and men are basically polygamous and this causes constant conflict between the sexes.

I suppose one should come to terms with this but I find it difficult to do so'.

Another girl, this time a twenty-year-old, said: 'In a way I resent men because they are so often inconsiderate. I also resent the way they can switch their feelings on and off whereas I, as a woman, cannot do this. So often men use women like animals, just when they feel that they want sex regardless of whether the woman wants sex or not. I want a man to make me feel that he really wants me and that I am something to him rather than just another girl. I want a man who will be concerned about every aspect of me and interested in everything I do'.

Under examination these two statements should appear shocking to members of either sex. The hostility which these girls feel towards men at such a young age is awful, but unfortunately they do have some reason to feel this way. Both have suffered at the hands of insensitive young men, they have felt used, rejected and hurt and with corroboration from friends who have felt similarly their attitude is not at all surprising. The second girl has reached the point where she wants a man who will *need* her while asserting himself occasionally so as not to appear too obviously dependent, and thus unmasculine – the foundations for yet another bad marriage have been cemented in place. These girls – and they are representative of a fair number – are utterly confused and certainly a long way from achieving their apparent ideal, 'emancipation'.

In chapter four we saw how this cancerous resentment grows and breeds unhappiness. Its cause is a concept which has cropped up many times in this book – ignorance – not only ignorance of sexual technique but of the basic human emotion of love. Love is our salvation yet we fear it, abuse it and misunderstand its infinite diversity. Sexuality is a part of love, and perhaps at least if men and women could understand sexuality they may go on to understand something of what loving is about, and more people could speak as the following woman: 'As I have sexual relations with one man, I can only discuss him and he certainly is very much aware of a woman's psychological and physical needs. I know that I am very lucky to be married to him as there seems to be a great shortage of understanding males. Lots of men seem to want to use women for their own satisfaction. I know that many women are at fault too, for not trying harder to let their menfolk know what excites them. I am sure that with honest discussion and a determined effort to understand their partner's likes and dislikes more people could lead happier and more contented lives. It really is a pity that many human beings seem reluctant to do this. There would be far less tension and bitterness if people could open up and release their pent-up desires, providing that these didn't involve hurting or maiming other people.

'All human beings need to feel that somebody cares about them and we all have our own particular standards to determine whether this is so or not. I think that males as well as females need special care and attention as well as excitement for a relationship to remain balanced and stimulating. For me, my role as the feminine half is in caring for my husband, propping him up in times of depression or uncertainty and in being as sexually exciting as possible. I listen to my husband and try to provide constructive criticism. I try to help him understand my desires and depressions as well as trying to find out what makes his life contented and rewarding. There are so many things large and small which make or mar a relationship.

'Sexual morality as it is today is unbalanced. Sexual freedom is good, but more attention should be given to the qualities of warmth, consideration and honesty as well as to excitement and titillation. I am happy to accept the principles of the contraceptive pill as it gives me an increased feeling of dignity as a woman and equality with men over sexual matters'.

Thus, after all the talking is over and all the hours of interviewing are behind me, I can only make the same old plea, a plea for understanding and education, so that one day this book might become redundant. Its only value will then be historical and its readers will conclude that the necessity for its existence reflected a sad state of affairs.

Appendix: Fourteen Interviews

Mrs J, age 26. Occupation: secretary, London.
Education: grammar school. Background: Only child;
father died when she was thirteen; married for
four years and has no children.

My childhood was a particularly happy one. Father had a good job and we lived comfortably in a large house in London, close to the river. Mother was, and is, quite an exceptional person. I think she is one of the most relaxed people I have known. She is uninhibited and possesses a generous mind. Her influence on me was greater than my father's, since he was travelling most of the time and really came home only for weekends.

Nudity was never regarded as immodest in our house and my parents never made flustered cover-ups if I happened to walk into their bedroom. Occasionally, I saw my father naked, but he was not an exhibitionist and did not expose himself intentionally. My mother, on the other hand, who was very attractive, liked to be seen nude. In my early years, it was commonplace for me to wash her back for her in the bath, after which she would usually bathe me. In the summer months, she often knelt in the nude beside the bath to wash me and I remember admiring her breasts with their prominent nipples. Another source of curiosity for me was her pubic hair and, in response to my many enquiries, she assured me that I would be the same one day. Full of impatience, though, I thought the time would never come. I remember it was a particular treat for me to snuggle up to her warm body as she dried me. Sometimes, when my curiosity got the better of me, my hands would become too venturesome and then she would slip away, but with a smile, telling me to finish myself.

At the age of eleven, due mainly to the vague whispers of girls at school, I became inquisitive about sex. My mother, when I asked her, explained the basic sexual processes to me without once using the abstract image of 'the birds and bees'. In answer to my forthright question as to whether my father's penis hurt her as it was so large, she assured me that they were 'perfectly suited'. 'A woman is elastic', she went on to tell me, 'in fact, I should be sorry if he were smaller.'

At weekends, I used to be a little jealous when my father came home and diverted my mother's attention from me. I felt especially resentful on Saturday and Sunday nights when I used to hear the creaking of their bed. Once, I asked mother if they had been doing 'that thing' together. She admitted quite freely that they had been making love.

Tragedy struck the household when I was thirteen. My father was involved in a car crash and killed instantly. Poor mother, she was really heartbroken, and it took a long while for her to recover her smile and easy sense of humour. However, insurance and other benefits left us well provided for and we were able to remain in London, where my mother took a part-time job.

Probably, my strongest recollection of early sex concerns an incident which took place a year after my father's death. At school, all sorts of books were in circulation. Some were textbooks on marriage and the practice of love, whilst others were 'straight' pornography. One tattered novelette which came into my curious hands was entitled 'The Diary of a Nymphomaniac'. I remember reading it in the privacy of my bedroom, where my reactions were a mixture of disgust, bewilderment, disbelief and a degree of fascination. Of course, I knew what it described to be an exaggeration, it had to be. But I wondered all the same if it didn't contain at least an element of truth. Carelessly, I left the book on my bedside pedestal.

The following afternoon when I came in from school, the house had an eerie silence about it. I tip-toed upstairs (as one seems inclined to do in an empty house) and saw that my mother's bedroom door was open. Just as I was about to go in, I halted and peered around the door. I am glad I did, because there she was, spread out naked on the bed with pillows under her bottom so that her back was arched. With one hand she was fondling her breasts whilst with the other she stroked between her legs. As I turned away I saw the book lying on the bed beside her. My main reaction was one of sadness for her. Since my father's death, she had not brought men into the house, as could so easily have happened. Was it so surprising then that she should need to do this thing? I felt a little guilty myself for having brought the book home in the first place.

Later that evening, my mother cautioned me about who I mixed with and what I read. She said she had destroyed the book from my bedroom. I remember blushing, but made no reply. I was fourteen at the time and still wasn't sure how to piece together all that I had been told about sex, as well as what I had read and witnessed myself. Somehow, though, it all seemed to extend beyond the bounds of simplicity as first explained by my mother.

It was perhaps not surprising that my attention should now turn to my own sexuality. Sometimes I would sit in front of the mirror and admire my development. With pride, I saw that my breasts were already forming and that there was a growth of fine pubic hair. It was during one of the moments of self-admiration that I first masturbated. The compulsion to do so had come in the bath as I soaped myself. Wanting to contain the sensation as long as possible, I got dry and finished the self-indulgence in my bedroom. Emulating my mother's method, I tucked pillows under my bottom and enjoyed the upthrust position these created. There was little I needed to do before I found my head swimming with the kind of vertigo one experienced on heights. I was conscious of a slightly vulgar squelching noise between my legs, then the climax exploded like rockets in the sky. Afterwards, I felt very weak and, oh, so guilty! Before going to sleep, I reached for the dictionary and looked up the meaning of the word 'masturbate'. The definition was simply 'self-abuse'! This censorious explanation made me feel even more guilty. Going to the mirror, I looked for signs which might give people clues as to what I had done. Then I found myself resenting the dictionary, and consoled myself that what it really meant was 'self-relief'. That slight re-adjustment made me feel much better.

Up until the time I lost my virginity at eighteen, I had several juvenile boyfriends. Most of the sexual activity could be classed as 'heavy petting'. Some of the time, I discouraged exploring hands, but often participated in mutual masturbation. I suppose a significant moment in a girl's sexual education is when she holds a penis for the first time. I used to giggle when the boy came. When that happened his fight and ardour seemed to vanish, and what had once been a proud member became cowed. It was funny, I thought, that father should have been so big when these boys were nothing special in size. The thought relaxed my apprehension about

100

intercourse, which I now began to anticipate.

I first 'had it' with a very pretty, not particularly virile boy who worked in the same office as me. We got along well together and had many enjoyable dates. Mother had taken to going away for the occasional weekend now that I was grown up, and it was good to see her living again, for she was still an attractive woman. So, on one of her absent weekends, I brought George home. At first we were a bit diffident and perhaps, guilty. Gradually, we started to neck and, since George was not aggressive, I took the initiative. Our first attempt at intercourse was clumsy and unsuccessful. Just when we seemed lined up, he went soft, and, as I was having trouble keeping lubricated, I suggested we try a genital kiss. He was obviously reluctant, but I encouraged him by taking the first step. Eventually, we made it, and I felt no more than a slight stinging sensation. In terms of orgasm or relief, it yielded nothing. As the weekend progressed, however, we became more relaxed and less self-conscious about the mechanics of the act. Before George left, I felt at least my hymen was broken, even if it hadn't been the shattering or exciting business I had expected. Also, the guilt I felt was negligible, and far less than after masturbation.

George was a keen photographer, that being his main job at the P.R. firm where we both worked. Sometimes, when we had the house to ourselves, he would run off reels of film as I posed. At first, the studies were in clothes, underwear or plainly nude. Later, I had the urge to have some indecent exposures taken. We used to joke about these and say that if ever we stopped at Port Said, we could reverse the market and sell filthy pictures to the Arabs. Mind you, I made sure he handed over the negatives.

I suppose his greatest triumph was a picture of me in sensual appreciation before a mirror. I had my legs open and raised onto the dressing table. The reflective effect was stunning. George asked if he could keep a copy, saying he would like it to refer to should he have compulsions toward homosexuality. I agreed, thinking that if the sharp definition of my partly opened vagina didn't keep him straight, nothing would.

Eventually, George was moved to another branch of the company in the North and we rarely saw each other again. I suppose, in retrospect, I would call it a very immature relationship. You certainly wouldn't catch me posing now. But at least it eased me into sex without tears.

After George, I had intercourse with three men before I married. The first of these was probably the most important: it heralded my first orgasm. Funny, during those youthful jumps with George, I really thought it was the real thing. I had experienced some satisfaction, but it became obvious later that there were far higher planes.

Peter was a married man. Nevertheless, against my better judgment, I got involved. What perplexed me about the married men in my life was their urgency and need. It was as though they had been leading a celibate existence for years and were now making up for lost time, when, in all probability, they had had sex only the night before. It was during one of these first, urgent acts with Peter that I got the message. For the first time, my mind was also involved. His preparation work was good and by the time he entered me I was well and truly ready for him. I had never experienced that degree of anticipation before. After we had made love, he was erect again in a very short time and wanted me in a different position. Obediently, I rolled over and let him enter me from behind. Again, the mental and physical lines fused. When he checked his watch and pulled on his trousers, I suppose I partly understood the answer to my question about urgency.

The remainder of my observations all relate to my experiences and views in married life. These are really the ones that matter, I think, for they are set in conditions which should produce accurate judgements. There should be no guilt involved and a strong mental harmony with one's husband should be present. My earlier experieces I would call 'sex', the married ones, 'love-sex'.

To talk first about the elusive sensation called orgasm I am sure it exists in degrees. While pretty well every act of coitus is satisfying to me, every so often there is a 'special' one which is set apart from the rest. It is during one of these sublime experiences that I crash the sound barrier, and I don't use the simile lightly, although there is also a Will-o-the-Wisp, quicksilver quality to the experience which makes it difficult to recall and describe with any great certainty. By the time I have subsequently drifted towards contented sleep, the memory is already sketchy. Still, if one doesn't have even an orgasm of lower intensity, it is not necessarily fair, in my opinion, to blame one's lover. Yes, often he can be selfish and stampede the net, but, sometimes, it only needs a gesture to guide him towards your wants.

I have experienced double orgasm (and it has never been more) about six times, when the circumstances have been just right. The first time was after a party. When my husband and I got home, I was feeling tremendously tuned up, sexually. Fortunately, he hadn't had too much to drink and was still able to make love. I nearly hit the ceiling after a couple of thrusts from him. He seemed surprised but, after a pause, I urged him on. We then 'came' together. I remember lying back, elated at this new breakthrough: the mental uplift and physical release had been incredible. After this, I found that a party or an erotic film usually sent me to bed wide open and in a totally receptive condition.

Once, we tried to stage-act the business. It really relied on two factors: me being highly tuned and my husband being over-aroused. A couple of hours before going to bed, I masturbated him while he gave the genital kiss. Of course, I made sure I didn't reach a climax. While he was undressing, I stimulated myself in the bathroom stroking my breasts and fingering myself. It was a pretty good attempt. I had an early orgasm, followed by the thrills of a lengthy intercourse, before he was able to ejaculate.

On balance, though, I vote higher the spontaneous act. Orgasm must be terribly important in a woman's love-making, because it is the mental release which signals that the act has been a joy and an exhilarating physical success. I don't think it's just physical caresses that stimulate one to achieve orgasm. I feel also that the woman has to be on the same mental wave-length as her lover. What he says can, and does, provide this kind of communication. If at the same time, it is plainly you he wants, and you alone, this in itself can suffice. There are times, I must admit, when our language becomes a bit obscene during love-making. Usually, this happens when I am exhorting my husband to more strenuous efforts. He will reply in similar vein. If I should be in a modest mood and he swears, though, it could ruin the whole atmosphere. One has just got to be good at playing it by ear.

Lengthy chapters have been written in sexual encyclopaedias and manuals about gestures and skills that must arouse a woman. For me, it can begin at the kitchen sink, with my husband pressing from behind and fondling my breasts. When we go to bed, I invariably sit on my husband's knee while his hands stroke my nipples and vagina. I find it comforting to feel his erect penis against my bottom. Then again, I enjoy the sit-up-in-bed exchanges. This gives a chance to suck my nipples as I brush my fingers against his. I always make sure to let him see my vagina, which consistently encourages him into a genital kiss.

Generally speaking, the sight of a firm erection is exciting to me. When I read of the controversy about size, I believe the erotic effect of a substantial 'hard' is overlooked. My earlier boyfriend's penis was a lot smaller than my husband's and it never aroused me to the same animal force that I now relish. True, the degree of friction on the clitoris may be the same no matter what the dimensions are, but how many women have known the disaster of a small penis jerking out near climax? It can be shattering. When you are moving violently in the throes of a big physical response, my experience is that you need all the length available to keep you coupled.

The one thing I have always kept well clear of is flagellation. I neither want to whip my partner, nor do I wish to be a masochist. Love slaps are quite different, and these we exchange in good humour. But the prospect of the infliction of severe pain is abhorrent to me. My husband and I have no stated code of limits, sexually, but we do have an instinct for knowing what is unacceptable. Once, my husband made a move toward anal intercourse, but I deterred him. Maybe it was a fear of physical damage rather than moral scruples, but, either way, it's not for me.

I'm not a particular kinky woman, but I do possess a certain theatrical sense. I'd like to record a masquerade my husband and I once staged for ourselves. My costume consisted of boots, a blonde wig, bikini pants and bra. My husband wore a mask. He chased me around the house before laying me on the living room settee. His special surprise came when, on ripping off my pants, he discovered that I had shaved off my pubic hair. The whole charade created for us a stimulating illusion of adultery.

Since my first thrills at self-indulgence, I have masturbated fairly regularly. Now that I am married, I don't need to do it for pure relief. I can now enjoy it. Invariably, the impulse will hit me about twice a month when I am alone in the house. The first flush of anticipation is succulent. Then the stripping routine adds to my headlines, followed by the abandoned freedom of nudity. I concentrate most of my attention on my nipples as I sit cross-legged on the floor. Surprisingly, I don't always bother to finish. It is the first few minutes which are so important. I have never used equipment, such as an artificial penis, mainly because I have never had access to the paraphernalia. My husband had never believed that woman masturbated and, to satisfy his curiosity, I have done it with him watching a few times. During my period, he masturbates at least once during the week, and this makes me feel less guilty and more normal about my own activity.

On the subject of lesbianism, my knowledge is very peripheral, and was gleaned from the illicit library of the fifth-form at school. The name of the work of reference was I believe, 'Love on the Isle of Lesbos', and it came under the heading of mythology. It described mainly the cavortings of lascivious ladies in marble halls and their wallowings in communal baths filled with the milk of asses. I imagine contemporary homosexuality to be more neurotic than playful, however, and have no conscious attraction towards women myself. At the same time, I have not the revulsion I have observed among some girls when the subject is mentioned. They have genuinely shuddered at the thought. If I did ever want a physical experience with another woman, it would possibly be with a comely matron figure. The hard-faced 'butch' type could never appeal to me. On the few occasions I have been approached, say, at a party, I have teased the suitor, but then left it at that.

I don't think that men really understand the psychological needs of a woman. When they are trying very hard to woo, with bed as the objective, they can turn on the charm. But they tend to become lazy when they know they can get what they want. Flattery matters to a woman. It doesn't have to be a pack of lies. Quite simple observations about her hair or perfume can be adequate attention. It just confirms to her that she has been noticed. Before going to bed, it helps so much if a few words or gestures are used as a prelude. This business of having your nightie lifted and starting cold can be very off-putting, particularly when you know he's using you as a sedative because he can't get to sleep. Fortunately, I don't get much of this treatment, which is why I am so aware of the attitude when it does happen.

I would say that men are often more aware of the physical needs of a woman, if only because they are more evident. Anyway, a woman is likely to be more definitive about a certain action she may like or dislike simply because she cannot reveal her mental needs so specifically. In an attempt to do just that, I can only say that I want to be told my husband loves and needs me. Actually, I am prepared to settle for 'needs'.

In terms of my role as a woman, I see myself as a co-partner in marriage and not as a subservient factor. I do, however, respect my husband's masculinity, looking towards him for shelter and protection, which is really how it all began. In answer to the 'jackpot' question: 'Is it possible for a woman to be self-sufficient?', my immediate response is, 'Does she want to be?' I think there is a vast difference between reasonable independence coupled with equality, and self-sufficiency. Emotionally, women look toward men for security and solace. However strong-minded a female may be, she could feel inadequate without this umbrella. Full emancipation is so far advanced that whatever a woman may want from life is there for the taking, that is, in terms of career and status. Even Amazon-minded women who have risen to the top in politics or the professions have husbands in the background. You realise that 'self-suffiency' implies a total adequacy in every respect: sustenance of life and procreation. Even if we assume that scientists will eventually be able to manufacture sperm in the laboratory, do you think that this mode of conception will be emotionally acceptable? My mind revolts at the prospect of such a clinical society.

Females may like to assert themselves, but, when it comes to mating they invariably revert to the passive role. Whenever I have taken the active, top position in sex, it has been for the novelty value only. The sense of fulfilment has never been the same. Personally, I am quite content with the status quo.

Mrs. W, age 29. Brought up in Cambridgeshire and now lives in Buckinghamshire. University education. Background: only child of middle-class parents; married for six years and has two children.

I made up my mind at the age of nine that boys were extremely attractive and much preferable to girls. My parents didn't mention sex to me and at the age of twelve after a biology lesson on the human reproductive system I ran home excitedly to tell them how babies were born. I always had the impression that my mother was 'anti-sex', she couldn't bear men to look at her and didn't like it when they began to look at me. I often wonder how my mother and father came to produce me!

According to the rules of psychology my upbringing should have given me all sorts of inhibitions, but I haven't been aware of them consciously, although I am almost certain that unconsciously I was affected. When I began to go out with boys my mother issued vague warnings about what I may and may not do, but she never mentioned anything specifically.

I was eleven years old when I started my periods. I had been told about menstruation a few months before it happened. I went into hospital with a 'grumbling appendix' and the doctors thought that it may be connected with the fact that I was almost due to begin menstruation. I was scared stiff. I have always had a horror of things connected with the functioning of the genital area. I can remember that when I was extremely young my mother gave me what I suppose was an enema . . . I can't remember much, except that she held me down on a table. I wasn't ever scared of pain anywhere else, but the thought of having anything such as an operation performed internally around the vagina really frightened me.

I always thought that part of me was especially delicate and any interference, even from doctors, would be painful. When I went into hospital they took samples and scrapings etc., and told me it wouldn't hurt, but it always did.

By the time that I was fourteen I had started going out with boys. My mother knew about this because we lived in a small village where it was impossible to be secretive. After a while, I took up with a steady boyfriend. He was older than me, and very keen to make love, but at that stage, apart from anything else, I thought that to do so was morally wrong. We only went as far as light petting and kissing. At the time I believed absolutely in the idea that one should remain a virgin until marriage. I think that I came to this conclusion through reading. I used to read a lot, especially old books and of course they conveyed this point of view. I also used to read women's magazines which always gave the same advice to a girl thinking of sleeping with her boy friend . . . 'don't'.

Eventually I went to university and, much to my surprise, I remained a virgin. I would very much have liked to have made love with the boyfriend I had at the time but we always just stopped short. We went together for three years and planned to get married. However, I was too afraid to have sex because I thought that it would hurt. I was also afraid of getting pregnant which is what happened to a couple of my unmarried friends.

It was fear as opposed to moral values which prevented me from having intercourse at this time. My boyfriend didn't want an unwanted child any more than I did and ten years ago you couldn't really trust contraceptives. I could never have faced my parents with the news that I was pregnant. After all, I was their only child and they had built their whole life around me. I felt that I had to live up to what they expected of me.

My boyfriend and I broke up. He decided that after all I wasn't suitable and looking back I can see that if we had got married it wouldn't have worked. I was upset at the time and my reaction was to go a bit wild and I went out with any men who looked at me. I used to have sexual relationships but I would never allow them to go as far as actual intercourse. Then I met Chester, who is now my husband. I was still on the rebound from my university boyfriend. The night before my twenty-second birthday I finally had intercourse.

I wasn't in love with him but I thought that I was getting so old that it was about time I let it happen. He was as inexperienced as I was, but we clung together for mutual comfort because he was rather lonely too. Even though I was still scared of getting pregnant, I was still able to enjoy that first experience. It wasn't particularly painful. I didn't think that it was absolutely marvellous, but then I never expected it to be out of this world. I had known orgasm previously through manual stimulation, but had never felt that to be completely satisfactory. Of course, the deep petting I had had with other men meant that intercourse wasn't a completely new experience . . . I suppose that all it was, was technically finishing off.

Chester and I didn't exactly live together, but we both had flats and usually spent the night either at my flat or his. It always seemed rather odd to me that despite the fact I had felt that I had been in love two or three times I had never allowed the men to have intercourse with me, whereas with this man, whom I hardly knew, it just happened.

Eventually Chester asked me to marry him and I agreed. By this time, I was very much in love with him but I wasn't at all starry-eyed. We had begun with having one or two interests in common and progressed from there. We spent a lot of time talking.

A year after our marriage we had our first child. We had never used any form of contraception other than coitus interruptus. Our love-making wasn't particularly sophisticated or experimental. During pregnancy we made love as usual, but after having the baby I felt differently towards sex, because I had lost a lot of my inhibitions. I am sure that having a baby must be good for women in this way because it involves so many examinations and so much open discussion about things connected with sex.

In the hospital ward the women talked about their husbands and eventually got round to talking about sex. All privacy is abandoned; you almost feel as if your body isn't your own any more, that it's been taken over. Certainly, I have found that with young friends of mine, after they have been in hospital and had a baby they seem able to talk about sex more easily and frankly. Once you have been examined by umpteen doctors and nurses . . . bottom up and a quick swab down, etc., you don't seem to care any more. Until my first child I had always been very shy about sex. I couldn't have discussed sex with anyone else but my husband, nor watched a film or television programme concerning sex with anyone else but him.

I had a very grim delivery and it took me about a year to recover from having the baby. I was always so tired that I never felt much like making love at night, so I wasn't really able to take advantage of my loss of inhibition.

I don't remember much about what sex was like in between my first and second baby. It just went on without my being all that interested. After the second child, we felt that we had the family we wanted, but since we had never used contraceptives, we were somewhat stuck. I had reached the stage where I couldn't face having any more children because the second birth had also been difficult. I thought that I would kill myself if I got pregnant again. I realised that if we didn't do something about it, my whole life would be spent having a baby, spending a year recovering, and then having another . . . *ad infinitum*. I became so worried about this that I couldn't bear to have sex. I tried the Pill but I discovered that I had some strange psychological block which prevented me from remembering to take it each day. I have never been able to account for this, but I found that whenever I went to take my pill something would intervene. After the trial period I just couldn't trust myself to take the Pill every day without fail so I abandoned the idea.

The staff clinic I attended for contraceptive advice was reluctant to allow me to have an inter-uterine device. Of course, there was also the problem of having never known any kind of contraceptive, added to which was my horror of internal interference. I couldn't bear the thought of a diaphragm; it would have put me off sex for life. My nervousness over such things meant that it was years and years before I would even consider the use of tampons during menstruation.

As far as I was concerned the only answer was sterilisation, but this was some years ago and it was difficult to find a doctor who was prepared to go as far as discussing the possibility. I was lucky inasmuch as my G.P. happened to be understanding. He came to the house one day and I told him that I hadn't had sex since the birth of my second child three months previously.

I also told him that my husband was as desperate as I was. I am fortunate in having an extremely understanding husband but he is a very highly-sexed man and he was obviously under a strain. There was also a great deal of tension within our relationship. However, I personally felt no sexual tension myself; I could quite happily have written off sex for life.

I told the doctor that the only way I could save my marriage was sterilisation. He agreed and sent me to a specialist, but it was a further nine months before the operation was actually performed. During this time I was being sent backwards and forwards by the specialist who kept insisting that I rethink the situation as the operation was irreversible and if I were ever to lose my family, nothing could be done to allow me to have children again. In desperation, I had to write and tell him that if I didn't have the operation, my husband was going to divorce me. After all, he certainly had grounds for a divorce because a whole year had passed without our having sex.

I used to have nightmares about having babies. I felt awful about refusing my husband sex and occasionally I would relive his tension by masturbating him but I didn't like doing that because it seemed to emphasise the fact that we were not having normal sex. My husband was quite wonderful and would only ask for this when he was getting really desperate. I told him I didn't object if he had sexual relationships with other women, but at that time it didn't seem there were any available. Somehow we managed to survive. I didn't dwell on our problem so much during the day, but when bedtime came I always wondered . . . is he going to be able to sleep tonight or isn't he?

Two weeks after I despatched the letter stating that my husband was going to divorce me I went into hospital for the operation. Compared with childbirth the operation was a holiday. Six weeks later I had a final check-up and I was able to have sex again. Initially my enjoyment came from the knowledge that it was now safe to have sex and that my husband no longer had to be deprived. Later, I began to enjoy sex for sex. The children were getting older and we began to go out more which helped relax me. Looking back, I can realise what a terrible state I had got into, but at the time I couldn't get the problem into perspective. It was as if I stopped living for a while.

Things got progressively better after the operation and then I gradually went off sex again. I returned to the doctor and he said that it couldn't possibly be caused by fear of pregnancy any longer. He felt that the strain of the children was tiring me and gave me some tranquilisers which did help.

I still have periods when I am off sex and practically frigid. My husband and I have spent hours trying to analyse why this should happen and we have come to the conclusion that I am susceptible to strain and over-anxiety. Whereas some people seek an escape from strain through sex, I find that unless I am relaxed, I don't want sex. In fact, I have found that when I am feeling extremely tense, I can't bear to be touched because I am so sensitive, it is almost painful. At times I can't even bear to have my arms stroked. I ask myself . . . 'Why can't I, after all it's supposed to be soothing?'

If I do get into the kind of state I have described, I have discovered that if I permit myself to be physically overwhelmed by my husband so that we go straight into sex without the preliminaries I hate what I'm doing for about half a minute, but then suddenly it's all right.

I think that I am a sexual woman, but at the same time, sex isn't essential to me. I feel extremely sexual when I am aroused, but I also feel that I could go through life quite happily without sex. This makes my relationship with my husband more difficult because he has a high sex drive. The 'ups and downs' of my own sex drive put me on the defence and

I have to convince myself that I am as much a woman as other women. The present cult of idealising the sexual nature of woman rather than, as previously, the maternal nature isn't exactly a help to me. One feels that it isn't enough to look feminine any more; you have got to act it out constantly.

Over the past year or so my husband and I have talked and read a lot about sex. We came to the conclusion that because we were both virgins when we married, our sexual experience of others was limited. Thus, we decided that if either of us wanted to have sex with another partner then it was permissible. One night, after a party we held at our home, I decided I would put this into action and went to bed with one of the guests. In actual fact, we were so tired, we both fell asleep! However, the next morning I found that my husband had followed my lead and had gone to bed with another woman. For an instant, I was slightly shocked but then I realised that I didn't really mind at all.

Since this party I have had sex with four other men and my husband has known about them all. These are people whom I have met and found attractive as well as interesting. I don't just want another bed partner, I want a good companion too; sex is the least important part. I think that I feel slightly naughty and so it does have a beneficial effect in that I am probably in an unusually sexy mood when I arrive home, and of course my husband benefits from this. In fact, I tried an experiment in this way. I was going through one of my 'frigid' periods and so I rang a man whom I knew was interested in me and whom I liked a great deal. I spent the night with him and we made love three times. The next day I came home feeling absolutely marvellous . . . I was cured!

My husband also sleeps with other women and I don't mind, simply because I don't feel that I am losing anything by it. We indulge in our extra-marital activities only occasionally. The great majority of our time is spent together. I believe that it is possible to have many different relationships with many different people, each one being unique. I don't think that one lessens love through sharing it; if anything love is increased. I became very fond of one man in particular and I would say I loved him. However, it didn't detract from the deep love I felt for my husband.

I could see that if I had married this other man, we could have had a very happy life, but it would have been a completely different relationship from the one I have with my husband. In a way, it's rather a shame that we can't come back after death and live again, because obviously living with one person means that you go through a very different set of experiences than if you had decided to marry someone else. It stands to

111

reason that if you can gain some of the experiences with another person then you are broadening your own total experience. My husband and I discuss our extra-marital relationships and thereby improve our understanding of one another. In our case, it has definitely strengthened our marriage.

I think many women are becoming more liberated in this way. Contraception, especially the Pill, has led women to make the discovery that they can have more than one meaningful sexual relationship, although they are still in the minority. This will lead slowly to women adjusting their lives to their own particular needs and consequently they will be more complete as women. This attitude will mean that women will become more self-sufficient and combat the loneliness which results through divorce or widowhood because of total dependence on one man.

Mrs C, age 33. Occupation: secretary.
Brought up in town in North Lincolnshire
and now lives on an Army Camp. Background:
two brothers and one sister; married for
ten years and has four children.

My father went away to war when I was two years old and didn't return until I was eight. We children were brought up in a house with my mother, grandmother and aunties. My father was just a photograph on the sideboard.

When he did eventually come home, we went mad and would fight for the privilege of doing little jobs for him. I didn't know anything about sex and therefore thought it was quite natural when he made sexual advances towards me. Initially he would cuddle me and touch my genitals, but gradually advanced to cunnilingus. I never did anything to him, and he didn't expect it of me. I thought it was all marvellous, and we carried on until I was fourteen years old. I suppose in a way I realised it wasn't quite right, because I remember when I was eleven, he wouldn't give me the money to go to the cinema, and I said, 'if you don't give me the money, I shall tell mummy what you do to me'. For me to have said this must have meant that I understood I was my mother's rival.

When I was fourteen, he tried to have sexual intercourse with me and I was terrified. I didn't mind what he did to me providing I was passive, but I saw having intercourse as involving an active part for me. Also I was frightened it would hurt. We were in the house alone together, and I ran out and stayed at a friend's until I knew my mother would be home. After that, I wouldn't let my father come near me.

I have never felt guilty about what went on between myself and my father, yet I have felt embarrassed about it. Until this interview, I have never spoken of it to anyone. My father is old and ill now and needs his family. There would be no use in telling my brothers and sisters. I think children know instinctively when to keep their mouths shut about things. For example, I knew about an affair my father had with another woman, but I couldn't tell my mother. I am not sure to this day whether or not my mother knows about my relationship with my father. It is possible she does know, but has never said anything, because she is one of these women who runs away from problems and pretends they don't exist. When I was sixteen and about to marry because I was pregnant, she shut herself away for three days and refused to discuss the matter.

I had my suspicions my mother was frigid, although I think she gave my father sex whenever he wanted. It wouldn't have mattered how much sex she had offered him. It wouldn't have been the kind he wanted. He was interested in very young girls. We went on a coach outing once, and my father sat on the back seat between my friend and myself. When my friend and I got off the coach, we compared notes about what he had done to us.

As I grew older, I began to realise this attitude he had towards young girls was a bit sick, and I often wondered what would happen to him if he were found out. After he tried to have intercourse with me, I only spoke to him when I was forced to. This was easy to do, because deep down, he preferred my sister. I remember once he got drunk. It was unusual for him to get drunk, and we were all quite worried about him. He flopped onto the settee and began to try to put the lighted end of a cigar in his mouth. I bent over him to take it away from him, and he shoved me away almost pushing me into the fire. He said, 'go away, I don't want you, where's my lovely daughter?' His 'lovely daughter' was my younger sister. Even to this day, it hurts to think about that incident. I thought how, after all the things I had let him do to me, he didn't want me, but would rather have my sister whom he had never touched. I came to the conclusion that was the way it would always be. If you give a bloke what he wants, in the end he doesn't want you at all.

However, I did have intercourse when I was fifteen years old with a boy whom I was courting. To say I was crazy about him is an understatement. We used to be together every day. The first time we had sex, I didn't have an orgasm, but it didn't worry me. Neither did it worry me that on subsequent occasions I didn't have an orgasm. I thought it was something which would happen in time. After a year, I became pregnant, and we decided to get married. I was glad to marry, because it meant I would be able to get out of the house and away from my father. By then, the tension between him and myself was unbearable. He was furious, because I wouldn't have anything to do with him sexually.

The year following our marriage went reasonably well. My husband wanted to make love to me often, but I only once had an orgasm. At the end of the first year, he was called away to do his National Service in the Army. He used to come home at weekends and we would have sex, but after a while, he just couldn't have an erection and was unable to make love to me. He told me that he had become friendly with a man, but I never suspected they might be having a homosexual relationship despite the fact my husband brought home photographs of his friend and talked about him incessantly. I was becoming rampant but nevertheless I didn't look for sex elsewhere. My husband refused to discuss his impotence. It didn't seem to bother him I used to cry a lot during his weekend visits and I got the impression he was glad to go back to camp.

He did his two years National Service and when he came out of the Army, he wasn't the same person any more. He was forever cleaning his nails and washing his hands or brushing his hair. He would come home from work in the evenings, eat his meal and then go to his mother's where he would spend the remainder of the evening. It was impossible to talk to him, because he cut himself off from me completely. Sometimes I would talk to him, and he would refuse to answer me and carry on reading or whatever he was doing at the time. If any of my friends came to visit me and he was there, he wouldn't speak to them, not even to say 'hello' and 'goodbye'. Eventually my friends stopped coming, so all I had was my tiny daughter and this lump of a husband. He wasn't a husband, he was a lodger. At the time, I didn't know anything about homosexuality, so it never occurred to me he was a homosexual. However, soon after I left him, he went to live with a man, and they are still together.

Eventually I took my daughter and left. I went to another town where I got a flat and started a job. I hadn't been there long when my health began to deteriorate, and I had to give up work. Soon my money ran out, and I had to seek help from an organisation concerned with child welfare. The officer of the organisation was extremely helpful and found my husband. He and his mother came to see me, and the officer suggested that my mother-in-law leave my husband and myself alone to discuss our problems. She wouldn't leave and in fact, my husband asked her to stay!

My mother-in-law offered to take my daughter. I couldn't protest. I had no money and no home. I haven't seen my daughter since that day. I try not to think about her. I have erected a barrier which prevents me from dwelling upon thoughts of her. I was at the other end of the country so there was no question of visiting her. A few years later, my father went to visit my mother-in-law. He came back and said that the child was happy with her grandmother and it was the best for her if I left things as they were.

Left on my own, I had little choice but to go and live in a hostel. By this time, I was half crazy. I went on the streets for a while to try and keep body and soul together. I didn't give a damn. I was quite convinced it was my fault my marriage had broken up and I had lost my daughter. I thought I was sex-mad and if that was the case, I might as well go out and earn my living that way.

The first time I did it, I was scared to death. I didn't really know what to do, so I stood around in the street for a while until a van pulled up and the driver asked me to get in. I told him that it was the first time I had been on the streets. At first he didn't believe me, but after a while, he realised I was telling the truth. He gave me a pound and told me to go home. I was lucky, because I came across a number of men who took pity on me and gave me money for nothing. The first man I had sex with for money asked me how much I charged. I didn't know what to say and guessed that two pounds must be about right. He took me up onto the Downs where we had sex. He gave me what I thought were two pound notes but when I got back into town and into the light, I discovered they were in fact ten-shilling notes.

Sex in these circumstances consists of gritting your teeth, shutting your eyes and hoping they do you quick. There is absolutely nothing exciting about it. I didn't get a thing from any of the men I had sex with during this time. I didn't do it for very long, a matter of a few weeks, so I only met one man who demanded anything other than straight sex. I went into a pub one night and met this really smart charming fellow with a cultured accent. He invited me to spend the night with him at an hotel. By the time we got to the hotel, he was quite drunk. It turned out he wanted to beat me with a coat hanger. I didn't like the idea at all. Anyway he got into bed and he was so drunk, he fell asleep, and I got out quick.

I honestly don't know how I managed to get away with all I did without either becoming pregnant or being murdered. I wouldn't consider doing anything like that now but at the time, I didn't care what happened to me. I thought it was the only sort of life I was really fit for.

I only got out of prostitution because I was offered a full-time job. The job involved being in charge of a sort of underground coffee bar which was open all night. It suited me well, because I was able to live there too. I kept taking benzedrine and alcohol and for a while I really enjoyed myself. It was the sort of job which brought friends with it. Many of the customers were students, and they used to talk to me about their troubles. For the first time in ages, I felt I was involved with people. Despite the fact I was only twenty-three, I felt much older than my student friends as far as experience was concerned.

I lasted at this place for about a year without seeing my family, except for occasional meetings with my grandmother. One day, I woke up to discover I had turned bright yellow. I had hepatitis and had to go into an isolation hospital. I was terribly depressed and refused to give the name and address of my family. I used to spend all day drawing pictures of coffins with little saws trying to cut holes in the wood. I must have realised I was getting into a bad state, so eventually I let the authorities have some information about my family. The next thing I knew, the whole family had turned up. They wanted to help, so when I left hospital, I spent a time living with my sister before joining the Army in an attempt to forget about my daughter and close the book on my past life.

Many women join the Army with the aim of meeting a soldier husband, but I found I got involved with a girl. At first, we were just friends. We travelled together and did our training together. We were together so much it eventually led to sex. I enjoyed sex with her much more than with a man. I suppose it goes back to the way I felt with my father. I was able to be totally passive. This girl didn't expect anything from me. Everything was given to me, and I didn't have to give anything back. We were separated after about six months when I was posted to Ireland. I wasn't heartbroken. We promised to write, but we never did. In fact, I believe she married soon after we parted.

It never occurred to me I might be a homosexual, rather I felt I was bisexual. Even now, although I am married and the mother of four children, there are times when I get quite desperate and at these times, I think the only thing to do is to meet a woman. I would never go as far as to go out and look for a woman. I think it is definitely true a woman knows what another woman wants as far as love-making is concerned, whereas most men are only bent on one thing, having their climax. Mostly they don't give a damn whether or not the woman is ready.

After I parted from my girlfriend, I met my present husband. He was a soldier too. I don't think I fell in love with him but at the time I needed

116

somebody. I am the type of woman who gets into a lot of trouble when she is single. It is much better for me to be married. When we were courting, my husband and I had intercourse. He put on a great pretence of being sexy. He was a virgin, and I thought in time our love-making would improve, but even now, after ten years of marriage, it is like being made love to by a boy who does everything in a mad rush. Although I have tried to bring a little variety into our sex-life, it hasn't really worked. When we had been married for six months, he told me that he didn't get any feeling from kissing. This remark seemed to be the start of the breakdown of his pretending to be a sexually responsive person. At times, I would caress him and ask him if it made him feel nice. He would answer no. He then reached the point where he was making love to me from the waist downwards, forgetting the top half of me existed. Now it is a case of him penetrating almost immediately, satisfying himself quickly, and leaving me high and dry. Another problem exists in that I can't have any more children, because I have thrombosis. This also causes complications as far as contraception is concerned, and sterilisation is the only alternative. It would be quite simple for me to go into hospital and have the operation, but I am too frightened. Consequently, my husband and I have had to adopt coitus interruptus which I find unsatisfactory.

I have tried to talk to him about our sexual problems. I gave him a copy of *Forum*, but it is still by his bedside unopened. I also tried to get him to a marriage guidance counsellor, but he refused.

I doubt if I will turn to other men, because I just don't have the opportunity. A year ago, I did have a brief affair. I was terribly frustrated which was emphasised by the fact I was working with 135 men! One man chased me persistently, and one day when I felt on the point of exploding, I gave in and invited him round for the evening when my husband was away. He was one of these men who can go on making love all night and he knew all the techniques, but nevertheless he failed to satisfy me. I think it was because his attitude to sex was so cold-blooded. He had no feelings of affection towards me. He was just a man who was performing from a book.

Sex without emotional rapport is useless to a woman. It isn't necessary for the woman to be deeply in love with a man who makes love to her, but there must be an affection between them. A man's sex technique is also important, but the fact of whether or not he cares about her takes priority. It is essential that men come to understand this basic fact about women. In my experience, I have found men know practically nothing about women. I have only known two men who realised the importance of making me feel wanted as an individual, as a *person* rather than as a female. Such men are rare, but it is easy to spot them. They have a kind of magnetism.

*Miss I, age 20. Occupation: secretary,
South Coast. Education: grammar school
and commercial college. Background: Middle-
class family, dominated by fairly intellectual
father; one younger brother.*

The only time either of my parents mentioned sex to me was when I started my periods, and my mother said, 'I hope you now realise you can have a child'. I became aware of sex quite slowly. I think I knew all the facts by the time I was about thirteen. I picked up most of the information from girls at school. It was like piecing together a jigsaw puzzle from bits of dirty jokes. When I finally understood, I was revolted by the whole idea a man could do *that* to me. I couldn't imagine it somehow. I just couldn't ever see myself doing it.

I don't remember ever seeing my mother or my father naked. They didn't try to make me feel ashamed of my body, but at the same time they never mentioned it. I was always my father's girl, because I was more intelligent than my brother who was less academic and more like my mother. My father had great hopes for me. He wanted me to go to university. I rather think he imagined me becoming a woman engineer or something similar. However, when I started going out with boys, I began to change my attitude towards study. It wasn't that I couldn't be bothered, but I had come to the conclusion one should be educated towards being well adjusted and happy rather than educated towards passing examinations. My father gradually realised I was no longer so interested in my studies, and this was a huge disappointment to him.

I think a great deal of the emotional strain I was under during adolescence was connected with the size of my breasts. From the age of fifteen onwards, my breasts began to grow larger and larger. I got to the point I was so conscious of them, I wouldn't even go to school. I had always been a plump child, but by the time I was sixteen years old, my bust measurement was forty-two inches. I talked to my parents about it, and my mother tried hard to keep me on a diet, but for some reason, I could never stick to it. I became hypersensitive about my breasts and felt people were always talking about the way I looked. It was awful, because I couldn't walk down the street without people passing remarks. This complex inhibited me terribly and was probably the root cause of all my depressions.

It was just before this period, when I was about thirteen, I first became aware of sexual feelings within myself. I was kissing a boy when all of a sudden I found I quite liked it. Up until then, I had always found I was somewhat revolted when boys kissed me. Eventually, I accepted the idea it was quite pleasant, although I still didn't like the idea of sex.

I am not at all sure how I acquired this revulsion. I think it had something to do with the idea of the male genital organs which I didn't find at all attractive. I have always had a lot of difficulty in bringing myself to be able to touch the male genital organs. I'm not sure, but I think I have always felt the penis is dirty, as much as I have associated sex with dirt. Despite the fact I never masturbated during my teens, I don't think I have had this feeling about my own genitals.

By the time I was sixteen, there was so much conflict between myself and my parents, I decided the best plan was for me to go away and live independently. So I ran off. I badly wanted to feel adult and decide for myself in all matters, and at the age of sixteen, they wouldn't allow me to do this. It came into my head after I had a party when my parents were away. They returned to find a window broken. They were disgusted, and as a punishment wouldn't allow me to go out. We had a row, and I just took a few things and left. I knew they would think I would head for London, so I headed south instead.

I met a French girl who worked and lived in a coffee bar, and she let me stay there. In retrospect, I can see she was a nymphomaniac, because she had a different man every night. We slept in the same room and I could hear her making love. It didn't excite me, but it made me curious. I began to connect sex with the idea of growing up. By then, I had already made up my mind I was going to lose my virginity to a stranger. I had heard all the stories about girls who fell in love with the first boy with whom they had sex, and I wanted to prove myself different.

One night, a friend of one of my French friend's boyfriends came into the coffee bar and asked if he could stay overnight. I found him quite attractive, so I let him make love to me. It was all rather miserable because while I was in bed with him, the French girl was having a row with her boyfriend.

I wasn't at all sexually excited and just lay there completely passive. I thought the whole thing was rather sordid, but I wasn't expecting very much, so I wasn't particularly disappointed. It hurt and I bled. It was pretty much the way I had expected it to be. The point is, I didn't want to go through the messy business of losing my virginity with someone I liked an awful lot.

In a way, I regarded virginity as an encumbrance. There were some girls at school who were extremely promiscuous and in a way I admired them. I didn't like the fact they would sleep with absolutely anyone, but I envied their freedom and their 'don't give a damn' attitude. I don't think the manner in which I lost my virginity had any subsequent effect on my sex-life, because I never regarded it as part of my sex-life. I adopted a purely clinical attitude towards it. It was an obstacle which had to be overcome.

Eventually, after two weeks I went home. My 'O' level results were due to come through, and I realised without them, I couldn't get a decent job. On returning home, I realised I hurt my parents more than I ever thought possible, and I was extremely sorry about it. Their attitude changed completely, and I was allowed to do more or less what I wanted and go my own way.

I was shocked by the fact my father was so hurt. I hadn't thought he was capable of being upset, probably because I had made such an idol out of him. I felt just as I had done when at the age of thirteen I found a copy of *Lady Chatterley's Lover* in his pocket. I hadn't read it myself and from what I had heard, it was just a dirty book. I was utterly shocked. I had never thought of my parents as having sex and, on finding this book, my father fell off his pedestal.

Soon after I returned home, I began to go out with a Turkish boy. I found him attractive and, as by then I had lost my virginity, I thought I might was well have sex with him. We made love, twice on park benches, but it didn't mean much to me. Almost immediately after finishing with him, I met a boy with whom I fell completely in love. My relationship with him was the most sexually satisfying relationship I have ever had with a man. I hadn't experienced orgasm and, in fact, I never did even with him, but I almost made it, and that was all right by me, because I was so much in love with him. Also, for the first time, I was able to have confidence in a man. I felt sure he felt the same way about me. This was terribly important, because I had always been convinced I was fat and repulsive and nobody could possibly care for me.

I don't know why sex was so different with him. After all, he was a virgin and totally inexperienced, but he stimulated in me an interest in sex, and I tried hard to discover what most pleased him. It didn't bother me I didn't have orgasms, because I realised many women didn't experi-

120

ence orgasm sometimes until years after they were married. I thought it would come with time. I would become terribly excited by him, but when he penetrated, I would go quite cold. I think fear of pregnancy was in the back of my mind. On one occasion, he used a condom, but I hated the feel of the thing, so after that, we always used the withdrawal method.

Our relationship went on steadily for some time, but eventually it began to cool off. We separated for a week, and afterwards, he didn't want to resume. For me, it was the greatest loss I have ever experienced. I was seventeen when I met him, and it is really only this year I have been able to bring myself to realise it is all part of the past. For ages, I lived in dreams of what had been. Twice I tried to commit suicide, because I didn't want to go on living without him. I was lonely, because I was living in a fantasy world.

I went to college in this sort of state and began to share a flat with a girl who was a lesbian. Her lesbianism didn't bother me in the least. In fact, I started thinking perhaps here was a clue as to why I hadn't been able to achieve an orgasm with my boyfriend. I began to think about lesbianism and the fact that so many of my girlfriends were attractive. I realised I had always been attracted to my best friend who is tall and beautiful and all the things which I am not. Whenever I used to stay with her, I always used to watch her undress, but it had never occurred to me before that I might be sexually attracted to her. I suppose my attraction towards women is partly constituted by envy, because I admire their beautiful bodies as something which I do not possess.

Gradually I began to realise I might be happier if I had a sexual relationship with a woman. I came to the conclusion I had to discover whether or not I actually was a lesbian, so I slept with my flatmate. It wasn't fantastic, but I took to it quite naturally. I wasn't particularly attracted to her, because we have always clashed on too many issues. I never slept with her again, but it was enough to tell me I was a lesbian.

Prior to that, I had slept in the same bed as my flatmate's girlfriend. We didn't have sex, but I can remember I lay awake all night because I was so excited.

I suppose, in a way, the time I slept with my flatmate was contrived and rather cold. She asked me if I would go to bed with her and I said yes. We took a bottle of wine up to her room and got into bed. I thought I had better do something and started stroking her back. She turned round and kissed me, and it went on from there. I didn't feel at all guilty afterwards, because it all seemed so natural, whereas with men I had always felt slightly degraded. However, I realised I wouldn't get any real satisfaction

121

from a relationship with her, because I wasn't in love with her.

I decided the only thing to do was to have an affair with a woman with whom I was very much involved. However, this didn't prove easy. I hadn't enough confidence to approach a girl I didn't know to be a lesbian and I didn't know how to go about meeting other lesbians.

In time, my flatmate and I moved down to London and we discovered a lesbian club. I was frightened and shocked by what I found. I couldn't stand the horrible butch women who were trying to imitate men. I am attracted to women because they *are* women and don't want a poor copy of a man. They were all so conscious of the fact they were lesbians and *outcasts,* and went out of their way to ensure they enjoyed themselves. The few people I met and talked to were so concerned about being lesbians, they didn't have any other interests. I began to feel quite desperate about the fact I couldn't find anyone with whom I could become involved.

I was really in a bad state and it was about this time I made up my mind to go into hospital to have my breasts made smaller, because I was still socially inhibited by the embarrassment they caused me. It was hell in hospital, but it was worthwhile, because the operation restored my confidence, and I really felt I could go anywhere without embarrassment. I made up my mind to change my life completely by doing the things which most interested me. I felt the operation enabled me to become the individual I so badly wanted to be. I became fairly self-dependent and stopped going out of my way to look for relationships.

Fairly soon afterwards, I met Jane, I invited her back to my place, and we stayed there for three days. We made love and I found sex was quite fantastic. I realised I could love her and had found what I wanted. For the first time, I experienced an orgasm. Initially, I had an orgasm when she made love to me, but now I have taken over the active role and have my orgasm when making love to her. I have found I don't really like being made love to. I don't think the 'butch/fem' idea is necessary in a lesbian relationship, but I have always felt having a man lying on top of me was degrading, because I felt this infringed upon my individuality. It wasn't so much the urge to dominate, but the *need* to have an equal sexual standing I could never obtain with a man.

I have been put off men altogether, because I have discovered, once they find out you're lesbian, they try even harder to make love to you, because they see you as some kind of challenge.

I have always tried to repress any animalism I might feel during sex. I have always felt sex should be clean and civilised and come in plastic containers. However, lately my repressed animalism seems to be coming to the fore. For example, I often feel I would like to beat Jane. Admittedly, there is a kind of surrender of lesbian love-making, but even now I am less inhibited, I can never lose myself completely. Perhaps I will be able to one day.

Mrs M, age 44. Occupation: secretary, London.
Background: working class family in Yorkshire; divorced
after eight years of marriage.

I remember having sexual daydreams from a very early age but I didn't feel acutely sexual until I reached my early thirties.

My mother never talked to me about sex and she forbade me to have anything to do with boys! I wasn't even allowed to be in their company alone. My mother died when I was thirty and my father died two years later. It wasn't until then that I was able really to act for myself. I was happy enough living at home, there were no rows, but when I was twenty-three I felt that I had to get away because my mother wouldn't let me do anything. Consequently, I came to live in London.

Before then I had had boyfriends on the sly. I went out with them because my friend did and I thought that it was the thing to do. I didn't read a sex book until I was thirty at which time I realised that if I had read such a book earlier, my life would have been greatly enriched. Until my mid-teens I was convinced that babies were brought in the doctor's black bag! When I started menstruating I thought that I had cut myself. My mother simply told me that from then on it would happen to me every month, but she didn't explain why.

Eventually I found out about sex through a friend of mine. Her father was a bookbinder and she used to read his books on the sly. At the time, I didn't really believe what she told me.

During my teens I was assaulted; I think I must have been about seventeen. I was in the park and this man came and sat next to me. He started talking about the weather. After a while I got up and said that I was going home. He offered to walk part of the way and before I knew where I was I was on the ground with him on top of me. He broke my hymen and that was it. I didn't know anything about rape and the law, only that if my mother had found out she would have raised the roof, so I didn't tell her. It was over and done very quickly and I was scared out of my wits because it was so painful.

After that, I began to realise that my friends were having intercourse with boys. At least they said they were, although I rather suspect now that they weren't telling the truth. I wanted to be in the fashion so I too started having sex.

I used to pick boys up in the pictures and on street corners. I was really no better than a prostitute. I didn't know what I was doing. Of course, because it was during the war there were a number of American and English soldiers in the town.

I would just stare at the men as they passed and give them the 'come on'. Once I had picked up a man we would go and have a cup of coffee and a chat before heading for the local park where we would have sex. These men never wanted to see me again, which was something I could never understand. I didn't find any of this exciting but I suppose it was something of an act of rebellion against my upbringing. Picking men up on the street came to an end when I read in the local paper that there was to be an attempt to clean up the streets. After that I used to pick them up in the cinema.

I kept on in this way without ever getting any pleasure out of sex. Frankly, I wasn't aware that sex was supposed to be enjoyable.

I met my husband at a dance. We only had sex once before our marriage, and were more or less forced into the situation. I took him back to my room for some coffee one night and my landlady came up and angrily insisted that I had a man in my room. While he was hiding, I told her that I hadn't and of course after that I couldn't let him out because then she would have known the truth. So, he had to stay the night. He got undressed and into bed, but I remained almost fully dressed and only got under the top cover. However, during the night he got on top of me and we had sex, but again I can't say that I enjoyed it.

By this time I had stopped the business of picking up men. I suppose that I just grew out of it. I had managed to build up quite a good reputation for myself and this incident with my husband made me feel terribly guilty. In fact, I think it was this sense of guilt which made me feel that I should marry him.

I only knew him for three months when we got married. I had come to the conclusion that sex was only permissible with marriage. I didn't love him. I can love objects but I can't love people because I don't trust them.

I did meet one man very much older than me, when I first came to live in London, with whom I fell in love. I had sex with him and it was satisfying and happy. He was the only man able to bring me to a climax, which is possibly because I loved him. He was very kind and gentle but in other ways he was nothing but a dirty old man. He would come and visit me and then go off to a prostitute. I still see him on odd occasions and we have sex. Sometimes he pays me and while this may seem shocking, it is more of a kindness than anything because he knows that I haven't got enough money.

He was best man at my wedding. I suppose that I really thought that by marrying my husband I would make this man jealous and he would come round to wanting to marry me.

At the time I was living with my husband, he was a violent man who was always causing rows about money. I am convinced that he is an incurable alcoholic and a kleptomaniac. Having a child made no difference whatsoever.

I was under the impression that fidelity was important in marriage so I never turned to other men at all during the time I was married. I became very ill while living with my husband. He used to beat me. One time he fractured my jaw.

We didn't have sex very often. He only wanted to do it dog fashion and I didn't like it that way. I used to have to bend over a chair and he would keep me like that for about two hours, I used to be bored stiff and would find myself thinking about what shopping I needed next day and things like that.

Now that I live alone I don't feel such a need for sex. I have made a friend of a lesbian but whether or not that will involve having sex with her I don't really know.

Miss G, age 23. Occupation: clerical assistant, London. Education: university but did not graduate. Background: small country town in New Zealand where parents both teachers; one brother.

I think because I had an elder brother I was always aware of sex. I remember being put in the bath with him when I was about two years old, though it wasn't until I was twelve that I became aware of any sexual feeling within myself. At that age I began a slightly incestuous relationship with my brother.

One day he began to talk to me about one of the women in the neighbourhood who was pregnant. It had never occurred to me to ask why this woman was pregnant, but my brother soon told me. Being young and naive, his information was rather garbled and inaccurate, but he gave me a general idea about sex.

125

On this occasion we masturbated each other and this happened again at odd times, but they were really isolated incidents. I felt guilty about it and I think he did too. Instinctively I felt that it was wrong because he was my brother and the whole affair seemed abnormal and unnatural. I don't feel guilty about it now, because I have since talked it over with a psychiatrist, and he said it was really quite normal. However, my brother and I never mention it.

My parents never told me about sex. I suppose my mother thought that if I wanted to know I would ask. She told me about menstruation but she didn't relate it to reproduction. I picked up most of my sex knowledge from books. In New Zealand it is slightly different from here because of the Maori people. In the country the Maoris still live in a communal way — there is one big room where the whole tribe lives. Even very young children are aware of the facts of life. They see their mother and father have intercourse, as well as their elder brothers and sisters. These people are quite without shame and therefore, going to school with them. I heard sex discussed openly.

New Zealand has the highest illegitimacy rate in the world and this is probably due to ignorance about contraception, rather than any particularly permissive outlook. I have noticed that the shops in England openly advertise contraceptives whereas in New Zealand that is unheard of.

I first had intercourse with a boy when I was fourteen and the boy was the same age. We used to indulge in heavy petting and I would get terribly aroused, so one day we had intercourse. I was very upset about it afterwards and felt very guilty about losing my virginity. I had been brought up strictly as far as religion was concerned and I felt I had done something bad. My parents had never actually said that sex was wrong, but I had picked up the idea from books and general Biblical study. I really felt wicked.

I can't really say I enjoyed sex, I got no particular feeling from it and I hardly responded. Yet, in spite of this and in spite of my guilt, I carried on having sex with this boy for about three months. Although it eventually became pleasurable I never completely enjoyed it. I didn't have an orgasm, but I got a kick out of thinking that what I was doing was illicit.

When this relationship ended I didn't have sex for a year. Then I met a boy who was four years younger than me and I had sex with him. However, I still didn't feel satisfied. I felt as though I had just been teased. After we broke up, I started going with a lot of different boys. But this didn't satisfy me either as I still wasn't capable of having an orgasm. I slept with far too many, about twenty in all. My only motivation was sexual

126

desire, and the fact that I wasn't being satisfied increased this desire.

I eventually left home and went to university. I met a boy who I used to go out with purely for sex. We had no intellectual common ground. We never went out anywhere together. We would just meet and then go off somewhere and make love. This lasted for about a year—we had sex frequently but I still didn't have an orgasm. I then left university and, after a spell at home, returned to Auckland where I met the boy to whom I eventually became engaged.

He was Vietnamese and when he asked me out I thought: 'If I don't go he will think I'm prejudiced.' I was a little frightened, but I went. Afterwards, he asked me back to his room and like a fool I accepted. When we got there he just threw me on the bed and held my arms down. I have this terrible phobia about having my arms pinned down: it goes back to the way my mother held me when I was a baby. When he did this I went hysterical. Then he started to kiss me. At first the thought of making love with an Asian revolted me, but I was so aroused I couldn't help it.

I kept on going out with him for some months, before I discovered I was pregnant (we never used any form of contraception). Soon after this I had my first orgasm. It was a shattering experience. I had this feeling that I was drifting away, that I was going up into the sky. When I am having an orgasm it wouldn't matter to me if I died — nothing matters. It begins at the pit of my stomach and spreads upwards, but it is most intense at the pit of my stomach. I have been told this is purely romantic nonsense, but it is true that the people I have had orgasms with have always been people I loved.

I think being in love with this Vietnamese boy and the fact that I was carrying his child helped me have my first orgasm. He had to stop me from screaming because we were in a hostel with paper-thin walls, but I just couldn't help it. For something that lasts only ten or twenty seconds, it's a fantastic experience.

Unfortunately I had to have an abortion. I begged my boyfriend to marry me but he wouldn't. I had to fly over to Australia for the abortion. It was done under anaesthetic and I didn't feel a thing. However my psychological reaction was awful. I had a nervous breakdown as a result of the strain I hand undergone during pregnancy and termination. I felt I was a murderer: in fact I still feel that. I want a child badly. Every time I meet a man I'm fond of, I want to conceive by him. I feel a terrible longing when I see babies, especially if they are Chinese or Japanese.

My mother found out about my pregnancy, but when she realised that the father was Asian, she agreed that abortion was best. I don't really regret it — I suppose it was the best thing to do under the circumstances.

I was under the care of a psychiatrist for some time. I just used to wander around crying out for my boyfriend. After about a year I received a letter from him saying that he was returning to New Zealand from Vietnam, and that he wanted to see me. When I received it I became hysterical with joy. I just cried and screamed.

The first time I saw him again, he asked me to marry him. I kept putting off telling my father. My boyfriend was at university so I only saw him about once every nine months. Of course every time we did see each other we had sex. This time I was taking the Pill. I think if I hadn't been taking the Pill I wouldn't have wanted sex, because I would have been so afraid of getting pregnant again.

When eventually I told my father about my boyfriend he was terribly upset and refused to meet him — obviously because he was Vietnamese. Then one day my boyfriend telephoned and said he couldn't wait any longer, and if I didn't marry him immediately he was going back to Vietnam. I told my father and his reaction was terrible. I just couldn't stand being so torn between my boyfriend and my father, so I took an overdose of sleeping pills. My parents found me and I was saved, but afterwards I was certified insane. My boyfriend's visa expired and he had to go back to Vietnam. He said he would send for me, but then he wrote and said that conditions were so bad out there it just wasn't practical for me to go.

Eventually, I decided it was no good sitting around in New Zealand crying, so I came to England. I arrived eight months ago and since then I have had sex with far too many boys — about twenty. I'm afraid I have this complex about not being wanted. I feel that I can make people want me for sex. For the past five weeks I have had a steady relationship with one boy, which makes me feel slightly better.

I didn't have orgasms with the other twenty boys. Sometimes I didn't feel anything. What I liked about sleeping with these boys was not the sex but the sleeping with them — having someone there to hold me.

I really do think that men are basically insensitive to women. The men I have known have not only been ignorant about women's psychological make-up, but also about love-making itself. For them sex is almost purely physical and they don't become emotionally involved. I think that even their orgasms are purely physical. Men use women all the time.

One thing which really annoys me is their double standard: they think they can get away with infidelity, while their wives and girlfriends must remain faithful. They resent it when their women become possessive. I think that men are basically polygamous and this causes constant conflict between the sexes. I suppose one should come to terms with this, but I find it difficult to do so.

Mrs M, age 33. Occupation: housewife, London.
Education: girls' private day school. Background:
middle-class family with three brothers and one sister;
married for eleven years and has five children.

I forget when I first became sexually aware. At maybe four years of age I remember sitting on the toilet and playing with my genitals; I can remember rolling the toilet paper into little balls and inserting them into my vagina and anus. My mother was always chasing me up from the bathroom; I can remember feeling vaguely guilty because I knew she knew what I was up to, though she never said a word to me.

She never has talked of sex to me; to this day if I mention the subject she fidgets uneasily and tries to talk of other things. I think my mother was probably a frigid woman even when young because I can recall my father nagging at her for things I didn't understand and she would remind him that the children were present.

I was passionately fond of my father; he died five years ago and I haven't yet recovered from his death. Throughout my childhood I have memories of being close to him; he would get into bed with me until I was twelve or thirteen years old, cuddle me and read to me. In retrospect, there is no doubt that his feelings towards me were rather incestuous; I can distinctly remember one incident when he was getting undressed to get into bed with me and my aunt came into the room and screamed because his penis was exposed. It could easily have happened many times before but I recall that particular time because of the look of horror on my aunt's face.

I slept in my parent's room until I was four years old because I had terrible nightmares and couldn't bear to be separated from my father. I used to call for him throughout the night for drinks of water, to be tucked in, etc., anything to get his attention. The only thing that shut me up was when he would get angry and beat my bottom with a leather strap he had hanging in the room for that express purpose. This was quite a regular ritual and I would receive a real beating, which I'm sure I must have enjoyed in some strange way, and yet as an adult neither sadism nor masochism has appealed to me.

Though my mother never spoke of sex, my father constantly talked to me about it. I was continually warned never to let a boy come near me, even if he touched my knee something terrible might happen. My mother had to escort me and my sister back and forth to school every day until we were in our teens, in case we were accosted by a man.

Both my parents' attitudes showed me that sex was a frightening experience with terrible consequences if indulged in, but this had no effect whatever on my early attraction to the opposite sex. Before I was in my teens I used to indulge in daydreams by the hour about romantic encounters with my favourite film stars.' I wasn't then quite sure what we would do together but my thoughts would so excite me I would shut myself away and masturbate. Interestingly enough, I didn't have an orgasm until I was about seventeen. It happened by accident and I didn't quite know what struck me; it seemed the room darkened and something hit me on top of my head. It's never felt quite so vivid since.

When I was sixteen, my parents separated; my sister and I went with my mother. My brothers are older and were living away from home. Once I was away from my father's strict influence, I really started going to town. I wanted to leave school immediately and my mother allowed me to without argument. I took a junior job in an office where I was easy prey for all the men there. I was very pretty, and I suppose vain, and was flattered by their attentions. I flirted with at least four of the men there and got myself felt and fooled around with in unused offices and cupboards during working hours.

During the lunch hours I used to walk down Oxford Street and get myself picked up. One time I met a man about fifteen years older than me who was an actor. I was attracted to him right away and talked to him of my secret longing to be an actress. He said he'd get me started and that we should have dinner together that evening. Dinner was at his flat, where he filled me with drink and forcibly raped me. It hurt and I was frightened, especially as he nearly strangled me to stop me from screaming, and my clothes seemed to be covered in blood. He must have felt sorry for me when it was all over for he helped me to wash my pants and slip and dry them before I could go home. After a brief period, the experience became buried in my mind and I soon was involved with another man; I was still not yet seventeen.

I suppose I could be considered a promiscuous teenager because I cannot remember how many men and boys I had affairs with during those early years. Neither can I remember any really deep feeling connected with sex; I wanted the company of men all the time, evenings out, parties and I loved all the attention. They wanted sex from me and it was, most of the time, something I gave them because it seemed to give me a sort of control over them, made me feel important. Perhaps I needed sex to give me an identity, an individuality, which I feel to this day I'm not quite sure of.

At nineteen, I had my first real love affair. He was thirty-two, handsome and with such charm he swept me completely off my feet. After a few weeks he persuaded me to go and live with him. At first, I wasn't sure what he did for a living, I was just so happy he had so much time to spend with me. I was doing modelling work then and my time was more or less my own. He explained to me that he was a professional gambler, which covered a multitude of sins. I soon discovered that he had a second girlfriend who was a prostitute and who was supplying him with the money he was spending on me.

He had such a sexual hold on me that I felt I was in bondage to him and grew to accept all the awful things I gradually learned about him. Two or three times a week he would give me a dose of benzedrine and we would have sex all through the night until I was weak and sore, and still wanting more. When he didn't have an erection during these sessions, there would be cunnilingus for what seemed like hours, beautiful torture, a feeling of hurting insatiability.

Sometimes he would phone a friend to come and join us once I was 'high' on the stuff, and both men would have intercourse with me; he particularly loved to see me commit fellatio on his friends while he was having intercourse with me. After a few months he introduced the prostitute girlfriend into our sessions; she and I would make love passionately to each other for his entertainment. I have never liked women, not even as friends really; I much prefer the company of men, but I developed quite a skill at making love with this woman and later, with other new girls he met.

He tried hard to get me to take on a few select paying clients. I fought hard against it but finally succumbed; twice I did it for money but this was too much to take and I left him.

I drifted for some months; a few casual affairs and I was drinking quite heavily. I was feeling very low, as though life had no meaning for me and I had broken from my whole family, when as if by a miracle I met my husband. I fell in love with him on sight and he with me; we both seemed to need the other so badly. From the day we met we have not been separated, except for the recent business trips, and I now have so many children to move around with us! From the beginning, sex was perfect with us. For the first year or so, we made love whenever there was an opportunity. No drugs, no drink, no extra stimulation, just wonderful sex.

We have always been close and have never kept secrets from each other about our pasts. The first few years of our marriage I think were something extra special. I personally had never met a couple as obviously in love as we were; and sex was always a great part of our lives together. The day I went into the hospital to have my first child, he had made love to me in the morning, which I think started labour.

My husband hadn't had such unusual experiences as I had had before we met and was fascinated to hear me tell in detail what I had done with other men and women. At one point, about five years ago, he became almost obsessed with the idea of having sex with another woman present. We carefully set about finding a suitable girl and indoctrinating her. At first, the idea excited me to think I could give my husband a new experience. I put on a good show, undressing the girl and kissing her and then inviting her to help me undress my husband. I went down, first on her and then on him and soon we were all involved in every imaginable combination. I was very jealous when I saw him making love to her but felt better after we had sent her home. We had three evenings like this but it soon began to dawn on me that she was more lesbian than anything else as she started sending me flowers and phoning me daily. We went to the pictures together one evening and she tried to hold my hand. It made me feel sick and I put a stop to the situation. My husband doesn't know to this day what happened to her.

We've often talked of meeting couples and changing partners, but I don't like the idea. I don't think he does much, either, but because he is much too intelligent and creative for his job, he has become frustrated, which in turn makes him seek new sexual thrills to relieve the tension. We enjoy almost anything verbally, but putting them into practice could create problems we don't need. We once brought a man home with us and I stripped to my underwear and he was ready to jump into bed when all of a sudden I felt I couldn't go through with it. My husband told me afterwards he didn't think he could bear it if I'd gone any further. Yet still we excite each other by saying what we'd do with another man in bed with us. Funny isn't it?

Very often we make love and I don't have an orgasm but I don't mind. It's his closeness and the meaning of sex between us that matters to me. Sometimes I tell him I've come when I haven't because I feel in some way I would be letting him down; or perhaps I feel I have to live up to a sort of sexy image I've created of myself in my mind. Our favourite, personal sexual act is for me to kiss his penis until he has an orgasm in my mouth and I masturbate at the same time.

I couldn't imagine having a secret affair. I don't feel I've missed anything sexually and a relationship with another man would only cause complications in my marriage. If I ever felt really compulsively attracted to another man I think I would have to have him before I got him out of my system and then I'd probably feel compelled to tell my husband about it. A very discerning friend once told me I have a longing to be dominated but a determination that it will never happen. I think in our marriage we have developed a perfect balance in who dominates whom and I think we both act out our personalities through our sex together.

Mrs P, age 27. Occupation: some acting and has private means; lives in London. Education: three governesses and private school; two 'A' levels. Background: upper-class upbringing by strict aunts in Jesmond, Newcastle-upon-Tyne after father died when she was eight and mother who suffered from a nervous disease died a year later. Six miscarriages and now unable to have children after partial hysterectomy; divorced.

To state exactly when I became aware of my own sexuality is difficult because sexuality and sensuality − at least in my case − must be separate phenomena. As a child, I was repeatedly complimented on my beauty. At the age of eight years or thereabouts I would spend hours in the seclusion of my room admiring my nakedness in the mirror. Even the breeze touching me as it came through the open window thrilled me. I was unspeakably excited at being naked and seeing and hearing men working in the avenue outside.

It wasn't until I was about eighteen, after reading certain books and admiring certain men, did I actually desire a man's body.

I wasn't allowed to mix with working-class people, and cruelly kept away from almost all other children. To me my parents were strangers and my governesses senile Victorians. There was no-one to kiss or correct me. Miss M, the last and longest serving of the governesses, convinced me that I could do no wrong but as I was a very shy girl, my sins didn't really amount to much.

I felt that I desired 'something', following an odd experience when I was about ten, but I wouldn't try to analyse my feelings at that time; though goodness knows my memory of every aspect of what happened will always be clear.

One day a complete stranger accosted me in the copse behind our house. He said something about my trespassing and treated me to a hearty spanking. I dashed home and shut myself away, shocked and excited. I told no one. Days later I ventured into the copse again, but found nobody there.

I began to play strange games in the copse; the sort I might play in my bedroom, imagining the stranger as some god or perhaps a father figure. Then I met him again, and again he led me away to a quiet spot and turned me over his knee. I neither cried nor complained during the tanning. This time, to facilitate matters, he took down my knickers. This made me feel that I could never face a man again. But, of course I faced him again. We met a score of times or so, often in an old hut in the copse. Each time I shyly accepted the spanking. One day he sexually assaulted me and I ran off, never to see him again.

Both my parents were dead by the time I was nine and I was cared for by relatives. People were always saying that with my looks I had a ready-made career on the stage but my aunts wouldn't hear of it. When I went to school I was still terribly shy and unable to take part in the many sex parties among my school fellows — though I was an avid listener. I didn't menstruate until I was fourteen and it was another two years before I learnt that intercourse wasn't solely an act for the procreation of children.

My old governess filled my young mind with prejudice and fear of men in general and sex in particular. I remember standing in awe at the playground swings watching the grinning lads look up the girls' dresses as they swung high. Paradoxically during the time I was having my 'therapy' in the copse, I didn't dare go on the swings for fear of showing my knickers, even to the other girls.

No sooner had I left school than my aunts began to match-make for me. I was still as shy and reclusive as before, consequently I was hopeless at conversing with members of the opposite sex. Fortunately I had my looks (people still commented on them, and I still had long bouts of narcissism in my locked bedroom). The fact that I had money was also an attraction and prospective suitors called on my aunts almost daily. I met countless types over tea but wasn't allowed to have a date until S. came along. While alone, he gave me my first real kiss. Within a week he was petting me and I lost my virginity to him within a month.

134

As always, I accepted everything that happened as inevitable, if quite startling. He was passionate and impatient. The affair was very painful, and apart from the exciting preliminaries, all I got from it were my usual shame and guilt feelings. I am sure a man with larger sexual parts would have left me frigid for life. However, he told me I was wonderful, that it was the great moment of his life, etc., etc., and bought me an engagement ring almost at once.

He called on us often and took me out every Saturday night. That night in every week, except when I had a period, he would make love to me between ten thirty p.m., when my aunts retired, and the time he had to leave for his train thirty minutes later. The pattern never altered, not even after a fifteen-months engagement. We were never anywhere near naked. My pants were removed, his trousers opened. I was puzzled, but grateful that he didn't seem to want to see my private parts. He was afraid about the exposure of his own. I got used to him and gradually looked forward more and more to Saturday. I became daring and a little bit cunning. Just before my aunts retired, I would go into the bathroom, strip naked and listen to his quiet voice through the door. Thus I was able to be ready for his ensuing onslaught. I experienced an orgasm with him only once, for he was much too quick.

After we were married, for a while things were very different. Although we had separate beds and never walked about the room naked, I began to desire him more. Stripping off our night clothes never failed to excite me, and even if our loving only lasted for two minutes, once every night, I was grateful that at least he had taught me how to desire a man. I thought that there was something the matter with me, because his love-making did not satisfy me. I must have been so naive.

In the third year of my marriage I met M., a friend of my husband. We began an affair. I was a shy, frustrated, young wife and he turned me into a real woman. Within a week I had experienced pastimes that were either taboo or totally unknown to me; new positions, spanking and symbolic whippings, cunnilingus, fellatio and anal intercourse. Since, I have never hesitated to indulge in any of these pursuits, if required by someone I have already accepted as a lover (even if only a lover for a night or an hour) though I must admit that the latter deviation could cause some embarrassment and possibly pain in certain cases. I didn't really live at all until I was twenty-two when M. took me right through the book one incredible weekend in Wales. With my poor husband I often felt so in want when he left for his own bed that I could have killed him.

Since my affair with M. orgasm has been fairly easy. This man taught me more about sex and about myself than many men could in a whole lifetime. I am now so sensitive that I couldn't visualise not experiencing orgasm when I make love. Approaching the sexual climax is like entering a private heaven. I have always been gratified and excited at my partners' orgasm – the most warming, most ethereal physical experience open to man.

With some men, one in particular, I can experience multiple orgasm. Odd though it may seem, basically I am still a shy person. When these things happen, the indescribable sensations are not exclusive of feelings of alarm at the sheer ferocity of the act. It is the release that is great. Orgasm is most certainly a combination of the physical and the psychological. I also believe there is a spiritual quality, especially in shared orgasm. I have been extremely lucky in finding one or two brilliant bed-partners with whom I have soared to unimaginable heights.

I am unfailingly stimulated by standing beside my partner or in his arms while he strokes my lower back and buttocks. I am almost too sensitive between the buttocks; a phenomenon that certain shrewd and devious young men have not failed to discover. Sometimes this has led to activities I had not even thought possible and that would be considered by society to be 'beyond the pale'. With one or two men I play the 'little girl in the copse' fantasy. With a good 'actor' my excitement mounts as soon as he says: 'Take down your knickers. I shall spank you.' Obviously a person as gullible as myself is bound to come in for some trouble and I suppose that I am lucky that this little fad has not caused me some serious hurt. A strap might hurt a lot, but the sight of a lover rolling it through his fingers is much more stimulating than the schoolmaster type with his clinical cane. Once I take a lover, I try to refuse him nothing, so the price of experiencing bliss is often no more than a burning bottom. Someone birched me, but I wouldn't like it again.

I have never had an orgasm by anything other than physical means, although I have often been stimulated by watching other couples copulate. Once as an experiment, M. held me while his friend beat my bare buttocks with a hairbrush. I had a complete orgasm, though I was pretty sore afterwards.

I can't have an orgasm through erotic fantasy, though I must have been near to it countless times. Often, when my husband left me high and dry, I would find myself searching for some kind of relief. Until I was married I don't think that I even knew what a clitoris was. I'd made vague attempts at masturbation when I was at school, without success. One night my husband had fallen asleep and I brought myself to a quick and totally unexpected climax. From then on, I was twenty-one, there was no looking back. Yet each time I masturbated I felt a tremendous guilt, as though I were an adultress. It became an obsession with me for some time, I shudder to think just how frequently it took place. I had nothing to do and all day to do it in. I had never been fitter in my life. The only thing wrong was lack of sex. I suggested to my doctor that I might be becoming a nymphomaniac. He hooted in derision. Yet twice a day for a schoolboy is claimed to be excessive . . . in my first year with my husband I masturbated, on average something like four times every day. I admit, I still do it, when necessary, for I now live alone and sometimes I am without sex for weeks at a time.

When I masturbate, I have two fantasies: I am pursued by a gorilla-man with a frightening face, into a wood (it's nearly always a wood). Somehow I've lost my clothes. He bears down upon me. He is erect, with an enormous phallus. He tries to rape me, but it is impossible. I come.

I am a child. It is the copse again. He is a gamekeeper or the like. He puts me over his knee, takes down my knickers and spanks my bottom, making sounds like gun-shots. I am crying and as I cry I have an orgasm.

Much of what I have said here has been told to a psychologist. He informed me that I was not a nymphomaniac, but highly-sexed. Neither am I a masochist, but merely anal-erotic. This is true, for though I can't deny the pleasure I derive from being spanked by a man, to be hurt in any other way, on any other part of the anatomy, would leave me cold. It is because of my visits to this doctor that I am able to discuss all this so easily.

After four years of total sexual freedom, I still think that it's all too good to be true. My need is for the relief and the pleasures brought about by intelligent mutual love-making. Any man I take to, assuming he is virile, is good enough for me and will give me pleasure. Penis size doesn't really worry a woman, though again I admit, one of my friends who is a genius in bed is also alarmingly well-endowed. Some of the greatest pleasures I have ever experienced have been during the long moments required for him to effect a full penetration. In spite of my readiness for coitus on these occasions, I fully realise that without all the wonderful patience and restraint he showed, the affair would have been quite painful. This is even more true of anal intercourse which we have had several times. Here his technique and control soothed my panic and brought about a union which I thought was quite physically impossible. He actually brought me to orgasm though I think that this was more psychological than physical: the very thought of his large penis being where it was had an aura of fantasy about it — though his hefty movement was anything but make-believe. I would not go so far as to say that this form of sex is necessary to me. I have practised it with three or four different partners, and although I have had orgasms, I have seldom derived pleasure from this act. I would say that for me it is the ultimate prelude to normal intercourse; the shocking animalism of being used by someone you can't even see, followed by the warm caress from the handsome lover about to possess you from above.

Fellatio would leave me cold but for the fact that it seems to gratify or stimulate men more than anything else. I find it more embarrassing than repulsive. Although I never complain or refuse, I get secretly vexed that they mostly get more excited than when having intercourse. Apart from the obvious embarrassment when an 'accident' occurs, it has been *finis* with some partners, leaving one with a sense of waste and frustration. As a prelude, however, it is pleasing, and with a partner's increasing virility and passion, quite exciting. Cunnilingus stimulates me but it is also difficult because I am so dreadfully sensitive in my nether parts. I have experienced orgasm a few times, with the same partner on each occasion, a middle-aged man. The sensation is curious since I can't define whether it is a vaginal or clitoral climax. It is also less exacting than orgasms achieved by coitus or masturbation.

I have often felt curious about, but so far have not had any physical homosexuality. Several boyfriends have wanted me to make up a three-some with another girl. Of course, if it is arranged I will play, but the idea is a little off-putting.

I have taken part in group sex. On a couple of occasions this was quite successful. By and large these experiments bring out my deeper inhibitions and I tend to become passive. I am, it will be recalled, narcissistic and once when two friends made love to me at the same time, I had multiple orgasms, much to the delight of the other four or five people in the party. This was the only time I have ever been able to let myself go at a sex party.

I feel that my role is to submit, wholly and unconditionally. I am grateful in having had so much fortune with my partners but at the same time I have worked at it. I suppose I could be called promiscuous. Although I enjoy sex as much as any married woman, unfortunately I have it less frequently. I have never refused a partner anything — the birching was a serious affair and left marks for over a year, one of the things that finalised my husband's divorce action — and have been re-warded with some warm, sincere friendships. I am not ashamed to say that the giving of my body wholly in this way has enabled me to enjoy a civilised relationship with many people — a phenomenon that would surely have been denied me had I remained married.

The 'permissive society' is mythical. Hypocrisy is more apparent nowadays then it was even during Victorian times. The Victorians tabooed sex outwardly and practiced (or thought) sex inwardly; whereas we pretend to support the emancipation of love, homosexuality etc., but in actual fact show our prejudices more than ever. I am sure that there is more dishonesty in people's attitudes towards sex than any other subject. Of course, children must be protected but I feel that sex education should be approached more intelligently. As for the adults, they have to go underground for anything other than marital text-book sex. I know that there is always the odd club or society, but should this really be necessary?

Mrs L, age 46. Occupation: housewife, Hampshire.
Education: grammar school. Background: father a
businessman; brought up in small town; married
and divorced by twenty-two, remarried at twenty-three; has a
teenage step-daughter by second marriage.

My parents never talked about sex in front of me and it wasn't until I had studied the human reproductive system in the biology lessons at school that I felt that I could talk about sex to my mother. Until then I didn't understand what sex was about. I knew about it through the other girls talking. As far as I can remember my reaction was – 'How horrible!' I thought that if one had to do that sort of thing to have a baby one had little choice but it never crossed my mind that it could be done for pleasure. We were lucky because we had a very good biology mistress who explained that when we got older we would find sex an extremely pleasurable experience. She answered any questions and helped us a great deal.

I began to become aware of my sexuality when I reached puberty. I was rather curious about all the changes that were going on in my body. I remember when I was about fourteen I went to stay with a girlfriend. When I was left alone with her father he kissed me. I thought that this was marvellous because he was an older man and I thought him very attractive. I don't think that I felt sexually aroused; it just seemed rather glamorous.

My school was for girls only and I am sure that this had a definite effect on me. I don't think that you are ever quite so much at ease with members of the opposite sex if you are in a single-sex school. I thought then that associating with boys was really a bit naughty. Despite such an enlightened biology mistress the general attitude of the school was strict and moral. I was once hauled in front of the headmistress because I had waved to a boy from the school bus window. She threatened to expel me if it happened again. A couple of years later my friends and I were threatened with dire consequences when we were discovered writing notes to our boyfriends during the break period. This made me feel somewhat guilty about associations with the opposite sex.

My parents always cross-questioned me. Looking back, my impression is that my mother suspected me of doing things which at the time I didn't even know the meaning of. One occasion my mother said: 'Never let a boy put his hand up your leg.' It had never even occurred to me that one might even want to let a boy do that. This rather shattered me.

When I was sixteen I went out with a boy who was in his twenties which seemed glamorous at the time. One night, we were at his home and he asked me to take off all my clothes. Although I knew all the facts it had never occurred to me that you took all your clothes off to have sex. I refused and left. I wasn't frightened but I was startled.

About a year later I met a boy whom I grew extremely fond of. He asked me to marry him and so although I didn't wear a ring we were unofficially engaged. My parents didn't like him and his parents didn't like me. I was also extremely possessive and because of various factors I lost him. I was so upset that I joined the Forces. I did have sex with him. We were left in the house on our own and it just happened. I didn't take my clothes off except for my underwear. We had sex about four or five times altogether but it was never too successful. He was terrified that I would become pregnant and refused to let me move. I had to lie absolutely still and he practised coitus interruptus. In retrospect I believe I should have felt at the time that it was unsatisfactory but I didn't. I was so in love and thought that was all there was to it. I had no idea that the woman should get any pleasure out of sex.

I certainly think that this affair had a subsequent effect on my sex-life because during my first marriage and for part of my second, I imagined that I was frigid. Although I enjoyed sex I always felt that I should be getting something more out of it. I think that if I had a full and proper sexual encounter the first time and been with a man who could have brought me to orgasm then I would have gone on in that way.

After I joined the Forces I met my first husband. He was about eight years older than myself and appeared to be very mature. We got married despite my parents' wishes. We had sex a couple of times before marriage and again, although it seemed satisfactory at the time, looking back I know that it wasn't. I didn't have an orgasm at all during my first marriage. I just didn't know what orgasm was.

This may have been why the marriage failed, although there were other reasons. Being older than me my husband treated me like a little girl. He would tell me off like a father. If I did something wrong, he wouldn't show his disapproval for about two weeks. This meant that things were always hanging over me and it became unbearable. He was sent abroad with the idea that I should follow but I decided that I would be happier without him so I never saw him again.

I met my present husband while working away from home. He was the same age and we had similar interests. I found him sexually attractive. Even now I find that it is sexual attraction which draws me to certain men even for the purpose of friendship alone. I felt that sex with him was much better and I still didn't have an orgasm. I felt that it was more satisfactory, possibly because everything else was well and I felt we were a good match. My husband had no previous sexual experience although this didn't bother me as I felt that I had learnt sufficiently from my first marriage to be able to help him over any stumbling block. In fact he didn't have any.

Things were fine until I became pregnant but after the birth of my child I ceased to be interested in sex. I could talk about it but I never wanted it. It wasn't until about five years later that I discovered the reason. It became apparent that I didn't really get anything out of sex because I hadn't experienced an orgasm. I discovered this from a book.

I had several girlfriends at the time and when I mentioned it to them one girl was extremely interested because although she had been married several years she didn't know anything about it either. Another just laughed and said that she didn't know how I could have been married all that time without knowing about it. Even then I didn't know how to go about achieving it. It intrigued me to discover that my girlfriend had an orgasm every time she had intercourse.

I thought that it was time to discuss the subject with my husband. I discovered that due to the fact that I would not permit him to play with me and especially stimulate me I was not getting a climax. We then experimented and it turned out that only by this means could I achieve orgasm. Today, I still can't reach orgasm except by manual manipulation. I had never allowed him to do this before because every time he had touched my clitoris I felt that I wanted to urinate and stopped him. Of course I didn't realise that this was a purely momentary feeling and that one got beyond it. One of the girlfriends had prevented her husband from touching her clitoris for exactly the same reason.

The first time I experienced orgasm I felt so marvellous that I burst into tears. Obviously this was what I had been missing all those years. I felt that this is what married life really meant.

Orgasm is for me a very satisfying thing physically and I think that it is purely physical in origin but I imagine it must be quite revolting to watch. I go completely rigid and suddenly there is this terrific release and I relax. I think that it only lasts for about ten seconds. It bothers me slightly that I can't have an orgasm during intercourse but I don't think it is possible for me. I don't always enjoy the sensations of intercourse; sometimes they are definitely enjoyable – sometimes nothing. However, by that time, if I have already had an orgasm, I don't really mind.

I have always had a slight distaste for having the light on when we make love. I think that this is because I do not believe that I have a very nice body. I can't put myself in my husband's place and tell myself that it is attractive. There are certain things which trigger off my desire for sex such as books, pictures and photographs, I don't mean pornographic photographs necessarily. I am aroused by photographs of half-naked women. I think this is because I identify with the girl in the photograph. There is a kind of envy in it. Obviously, many of these photographs do arouse men and there is something of this element in it. I think: 'How lovely to look like that.'

We have never used mirrors in our love-making and if by chance I ever catch sight of myself in a mirror while making love I close my eyes. In fact if we make love with the light on I close my eyes. I suppose this is because I am so self-conscious. We haven't ever used aids of any kind but if there was anything which could enable me to have an orgasm during intercourse then I would be glad to make use of it.

We do use imaginative aids. I think that anyone who has been married for some time has to. If you have been arguing about money or the children or something you can't simply climb into bed and have sex. We don't specifically look at books and pictures to arouse ourselves but if I have read an interesting passage in a book I might say to my husband: 'Look at this.' In turn this might make us aroused. I do fantasise during sex. For some reason my fantasies usually concern women, although I have never had any lesbian experiences. I imagine two women making love to one another. I must admit that I find lesbianism intriguing but have never been physically attracted to a member of my sex.

After I discovered orgasm I began to masturbate, mainly as a means of

142

experimentation and I found that I enjoyed it. Again, I employed fantasies and would usually masturbate after reading a sexy book. Sometimes I masturbate when I am with my husband and even when he is having intercourse with me and I think this may be one way in which I could eventually achieve orgasm in intercourse. I don't masturbate often; it seems to happen in cycles and for a certain time I will feel the need to masturbate fairly regularly.

When my periods were still regular, I found that I always wanted sex immediately after menstruation. I think that this was because I had a terrible fear of pregnancy and at the post-menstrual period, one has the least chance of becoming pregnant. We have used contraceptives, the Pill, sheaths and jellies but the only one I found at all acceptable was coitus interruptus. I never found this frustrating because I always had had an orgasm beforehand. I realise, however, that it must have been slightly frustrating for my husband and this rather bothered me. Now we don't need to use contraceptives it must be much more enjoyable for him. It is very important to me that he enjoys our sexual relations because I think that sex is so important to men.

I intended to have more than one child but the experience of childbirth put me off completely. To some women childbirth is perfectly natural and easy and afterwards, they are left with the pleasure of having a family. But for others, the experience can be extremely traumatic and can cause psychological disturbances. Compared with some women I didn't have a difficult time. I just thought that it was very difficult. I was absolutely shattered by the pain; I never thought that such pain existed and it left me with a definite mental block.

I didn't reject the baby but as a result of my fear of becoming pregnant again, I didn't want sex for a long time afterwards. This lasted for two or three years. Even when I understood the reason for my feelings and could discuss it, it didn't make any difference.

Before I had a child I thought that having a baby was absolutely necessary and as a result badly wanted one, but looking back I wonder whether my child is as important to me as she should be. It goes back to the old question of where does a mother's duty lie — with her children or with her husband. I rather think it lies with her husband. So many women put their children first and I am sure that this is wrong.

I think that it is wrong for a woman to shut herself up in her own little world and ignore outside things. As a wife, I must attend to my husband's physical needs such as cooking, housework, etc. and to his sexual needs so that he is glad to come home and doesn't need to look elsewhere. If my husband was unfaithful to me I would be hurt and jealous but I don't think that I would divorce him.

I have always tried to answer all my daughters' questions to the best of my knowledge and ability and told her that promiscuity leads to loss of self-respect and that she would become a very introverted sort of person as a consequence. I don't believe in saying: 'You must not'; I have simply pointed out the facts and dangers. If my daughter did strike up a relationship with a boy and thought that she considered herself to be in love and wanted sex, I hope that my reaction would be to allow her to bring the boy home for the purpose. However, it is easy to be dispassionate about this now but I don't think that it is possible to be non-emotional about one's own child, a point which may cloud my thinking when called upon to make a decision.

Mrs W, age 24. Occupation: nurse, London suburb. Education: nurse's training. Background: eldest of four children in working-class family in the Midlands; spent two and a half years in Australia; married for three years with three-year-old daughter and one-year-old son.

I suppose I must have been about three years old when I first became aware of the fact that girls and boys were very much different. The little boy who lived next door and I were discovered by my mother wandering around without pants on and inspecting each other. She was terribly angry and gave me a good hiding.

I learnt about sex at school but I didn't know the full facts until we studied 'reproduction' in our science lessons. When I was eleven and my mother was pregnant I was convinced that she had got that way through taking pills and nothing that the girls at school told me could persuade me otherwise.

My parents never mentioned sex. They made me feel very guilty about it all and I was never allowed to undress in front of them. When I started going out with boys my mother would say, 'Don't get up to anything'. She never explained what 'anything' was.

I came home from school once and asked her what fuck meant as I had heard the word. She didn't tell me what it meant but she did tell my father about the incident when he came home and he gave me a good thrashing, again without telling me what the word meant.

When I eventually found out about sex I was rather frightened. I think that this has something to do with me being intimidated by men, which is why I always give in. This is because of my father. He was terribly aggressive and I always think that if men don't get what they want they will resort to violence as he did.

I indulged in exhibitionism at a fairly early age. I remember being with another girl under a blanket feeling one another. Also I used to stand at my bedroom window with nothing on knowing full well that the boy in the house opposite could see me.

I was eleven when I had sexual intercourse for the first time, which sounds awfully young, but it wasn't really of my own choosing. My girlfriends held me down while this fellow, who was about twenty-five, had intercourse with me. We were in a barn having a laugh and I think that he got a bit excited. I was terrified but then I found that it didn't hurt, probably because penetration was at minimum. Afterwards I didn't really feel anything. I think that all my friends were fairly promiscuous and this was their way of initiating me.

After that I had sexual intercourse often with lots of boys. There was one boy I went with regularly and we would have sex two or three times a day in some air raid shelters at school. I never really enjoyed it because just as I began to get worked up he would finish. It wasn't really like making love — I was simply co-operating. I felt that I had to do it for the sake of the boys because they would get terribly aroused and then I would feel sorry for them. Even so, all the time I would say — 'You mustn't do it, you mustn't do it'. But in the end I always used to give in, and then I would feel ashamed of myself.

It never occurred to me that I might become pregnant until I was about fourteen. I still remember one occasion when I had sex in the grass with an Irish road worker and being terrified in case I got pregnant, but even after that I just carried on going with other boys.

When I was fifteen my parents emigrated to Australia and I went with them. I didn't want to go and resolved to get back to England as soon as possible. I twice ran away and tried to get on a boat, but I was brought back each time.

On the second occasion I ran off because my mother had found a letter I had written to my boyfriend in England mentioning that we had had sex. She told my father and he went mad and hit me. I got as far as Melbourne and was wandering around when I was picked up by four boys in a car. They took me to a farmhouse miles from anywhere. Throughout the night they raped me several times. There was a bedroom with four beds and they dragged me from one bed to another. The next day they took me

145

back to the city and dumped me. It was terrible.

I carried on looking for a ship but the police picked me up. Because I wouldn't tell them where my parents lived they took me to a hostel. There were all sorts of girls there. The first night I slept next to a girl who masturbated all night . . . going quite mad she was. Eventually they found where my parents lived and flew me home.

By that time I was about three months pregnant although I wasn't aware of it at the time. I had missed my period but put it down to the upset. One day my mother noticed that I was getting fat. That's how I found out that I was pregnant. My father gave me a good thrashing. My mother had to rip the shirt off his back to get him away from me. I don't think my parents ever believed the story of the rape.

By that time I didn't care whether or not they believed me, especially after my father hit me because I thought that I might lose the baby. My mother never really liked children despite the fact that she had four herself. Goodness knows why she ever had any. She took me to an unmarried mothers' hostel run by the Salvation Army, where I was only allowed out for two hours once a week. I had to scrub floors right up until the time the baby was born. I had the baby adopted (my mother's idea, not mine) and this upset me a great deal and even now I can't really bring myself to talk about it.

After I had the baby I started training as a nurse and lived in the nurses' home. The first time that a boy again tried to have sex with me I went hysterical. We were in a parked car and he started feeling me and took his penis out of his trousers. I ran off screaming down the street shouting 'murder'. I came to the door of a house and banged and screamed and the people phoned the police. The boy was charged with attempted rape but after I calmed down I realised that he had had no intentions of raping me. I went to court and told them about the four boys who had raped me and about the baby so they let him off. I don't know why I was seized with such panic. Maybe it was the fear of another pregnancy.

Not long afterwards I went to a party. When I have a few drinks I find that it relaxes me, which is what happened on this occasion. All the people there were Indians and before I knew where I was I was having sexual intercourse with one of them. I wasn't at all frightened because he was wearing a contraceptive. This was the first time that I had ever experienced an orgasm. I knew that I should have had orgasms before but the men were always too quick for me. I find that now I can obtain an orgasm much more easily.

I had another boyfriend who I used to frighten by making him believe

146

that I was pregnant. It seems strange and I can't really understand why I did this. Maybe I wanted a baby so badly that I enjoyed pretending.

Eventually I saved up enough money to return to England. I had several boyfriends and found that I enjoyed giving them an orgasm even though I again found that I was unable to have an orgasm myself. There was one boy with whom I had quite a lasting relationship. We planned to get engaged, but I began having terrible nightmares. It sounds silly now but I would have a dream about being on a bus with a lion sitting next to me. All the other passengers could get off the bus but I sat there with this lion licking my neck. I was really a nervous wreck.

I had other boyfriends too, but when I was having sex with them it got to the point where I used to wish that they would hurry up and finish. I was bored with them, probably because there was always so little emotional content in any of these relationships. Deep down I know that I was being used but I was always frightened that if I said 'no', then they would hurt me.

I used to masturbate often. I have done so since I was about six or seven. I had a ring and I used to put it in between my legs and play with it. Eventually I went on to use instruments, such as a hair brush handle which I would insert into the vagina. At one time I felt guilty about masturbating, but then I came to realise that it was quite natural. Sometimes when I am reading something very erotic I can make myself have an orgasm without even touching myself. I like looking at photographs of naked women, perhaps because unlike them I have small breasts. Also I like to imagine that I am them, having my photograph taken when naked. Another fantasy I had when I was younger was that I was tied to a post with men walking by feeling me as they passed.

Now that I am married I masturbate more then I ever did, sometimes every day. In the afternoons I get depressed because the children are almost always asleep, I have nothing to do. Sometimes I will pick up a book and read about tortures or something similar. This way I can get an orgasm without moving.

Reading about female torture stimulates me most; perhaps it has something to do with my being raped. It could be that I enjoyed it in a strange perverse way. Recently I bought a book about rape and I had three orgasms while reading it. My husband knows about this and thinks that it is funny. I don't have an orgasm every time we have intercourse and yet, and this is peculiar, I can make myself have an orgasm through reading almost any time I choose. I almost always masturbate this way because I somehow don't think that it is as bad as using an implement.

When I came to London I lived with a man whom I really found quite repulsive. I felt sorry for him because he was so horrible to look at. He was small, too, and I always feel sorry for small men. After he had made love to me, I would always go into the bathroom and masturbate because I was so worked up. He never gave me an orgasm and would just roll over and go to sleep. I could never have slept if I hadn't relieved myself.

Eventually we split up and I became pregnant again with a man who denied all responsibility. It was then that I met R. who is now my husband. He knew I was pregnant but was very kind. He didn't try to have sex with me at first which thrilled me in a way because my mother had always told me that if a man didn't try anything, that meant he respected you. I do think that R. was shocked at first, but he accepted it and stood by me.

We did have sex before we were married and I was surprised to discover that he was a virgin. It wasn't very successful at first but after a while things got better. I didn't let him know that he didn't satisfy me and it didn't really bother me because I knew that he hadn't any experience. I started taking the Pill but after we were married we found that for some reason it made me very difficult to live with. I changed my brand but this kind made me fat. So we decided to have a baby. Of course we already had a little girl because R. had adopted my first baby. After our son was born I tried another brand of pill and this seems to suit me.

I had to work on my husband because he has always been very shy. Just after Christmas I got him a date with a friend of mine. They had sex together and I was quite pleased about this, because my husband hadn't had experience with anyone but me and consequently nothing to compare me to. After that we were much closer than before.

One night I had sex with my husband's brother. I thought that he was experienced but found that he too was a virgin. My husband knew about this and went out so that we could be alone. I didn't have an orgasm nor did I enjoy the experience. When my husband returned we went to bed and I had an orgasm with him. It sounds awful . . . two in a night, but there you are.

For some reason this seems to help my relationship with my husband. He tells me everything that he does and I tell him everything that I do. We have been thinking of 'swapping' because we think that it is better to do this with married couples as there is less danger of involvement. I would like my husband to get a bit more experience while he has the chance. This would make him a better lover.

We don't really believe in marriage. We are convinced that if we were living together, it would make our lives much more exciting. When you aren't tied down in any way sex is more fun that way.

Mrs M, age 38. Occupation: research worker, London suburb. Education: convent school. Background: middle-class, unhappy childhood; divorced fourteen years ago after two and a half years of marriage; has a seventeen-year-old son.

I went to a convent school and had quite a good education, but afterwards I realised that I hadn't really absorbed any of it, which was probably a good thing because it meant that I had escaped indoctrination. Since then I have made every attempt to educate myself.

My parents were not practising Roman Catholics and were unhappily married. My father was a violent man and very brutal. He was unkind to both my mother and myself and this had an enormous effect on me and, in fact, still has, although my own knowledge of myself is helping me to overcome this gradually. However, I still find that I am unable to be affectionate towards my teenage son.

My emotions are sexually orientated. Unless there is a sexual element in a relationship I find that I can't function fully. I have not got the ability to love without sex. This goes back to my childhood when I had no affection from either of my parents and therefore all the affection I have ever received has been in a sexual context, even if I haven't actually had sex with the person concerned.

I had a number of sexual experiences during childhood. When I was eleven I visited some people in the country. Their son, aged about twenty, took me out into the garden. Suddenly he picked me up and laid me on the ground. Nothing actually happened, we just cuddled, but I responded immediately in a curious sort of way. It was a total emotional response rather than sexual arousal. It was a very vivid experience and I think that it awakened me to the possibilities of communication through the body.

On a number of occasions men exposed themselves to me. I remember one man who was masturbating in a park. He asked me to touch his penis, which I did. I was about nine years old at the time and when I went home and told my mother about it I couldn't understand why she made such a fuss. This incident didn't frighten me and neither did any of the others with one exception. I came across a man in a wood. He was masturbating violently, thrashing his penis all over the place. It was the violence which frightened me and I ran away.

I never talked to my parents about sex as I knew that my mother didn't like sexual matters. Whenever she started to talk to me about sex I would tell her to stop because I instinctively felt that her attitude to sex was wrong, as I have always felt that sex was a tremendously good force. Consequently I knew very little about the biological aspects of sex until I first made love at the age of seventeen.

I had known the man for three months. We were in his room, sitting on the bed cuddling and it just happened. It was his first experience of sex and the whole thing was spontaneous. We both responded to it remarkably without really knowing what was happening. It wasn't intellectual at all, but a totally emotional experience and very beautiful. I suppose there was some pain but I didn't take very much notice. I had a complete orgasm and felt marvellous. Later, our relationship broke up, but then I met him again unexpectedly and we were married within a month. It was hopeless from the word go but in retrospect I realise that our marriage floundered because of pre-menstrual tension.

I had been married for about two weeks when I got pre-menstrual tension although at the time I didn't know what it was and couldn't understand it. It made me quite schizophrenic. One minute I would be fine and the next I would be like a raving maniac, and there wasn't a thing to be done about it.

This, or course, caused arguments and we would have great difficulty becoming friends again. By the time we did, my cycle was round again. I would also suffer from tension for the two days of ovulation. This, along with the seven days prior to the period, plus the period of five days, meant that for fourteen days of each month I would be impossible to live with.

I thought that I was in love with my husband, but actually I wasn't really aware of what love was. I was excited by him simply because he was a very exciting person. There was some sort of magnetism about him.

He didn't really understand my problem or pre-menstrual tension. One of the ways I know that I am in the middle of an attack is that I begin hating everyone for absolutely no reason whatsoever. Somehow this hate is always directed at those closest to me. In my marriage I just wasn't interested in sex at these times, except during ovulation when I felt a great need for sex. At one stage of the pre-menstrual experience, you can discuss it and the way it is affecting you but eventually you go beyond that. Few men can understand this phenomenon. Even those who know about it and have it explained to them can never really bring themselves to understand it, simply because it is so outside their personal experience.

My husband and I didn't really progress sexually, mainly because of his lack of experience and because I found it difficult to be spontaneous. I didn't want to have a child although I loved other people's children. However, I realised that I am not very practical and was really unsuited for the responsibilities of parenthood, but nevertheless, I became pregnant within three months of marriage. It was too terrible for words. I suffered from tension for the whole of the nine months, and when they presented me with this baby, all I wanted to do was run away from the responsibility. The question of whether or not I have come to love this child is a difficult one to answer because I believe in reincarnation and therefore believe that he is a 'visitor' whom it has been incumbent upon me to guide and help.

My husband and I lived in a furnished flat and when the landlord discovered I was pregnant he threw us out. We lived with both our parents which caused difficulties. Eventually, my husband reached the point where he was violent with me. On one occasion, after the birth of the child he hit me and the baby began to scream. Well, I had been brought up in these circumstances myself and didn't want my son to experience the same. So I asked my husband to leave me which he did.

For a long time life was terrible. Although I had a flat in my parents' house they wouldn't help me by baby-sitting or looking after the child. I used to put him to bed, creep out and stay out for as long as I could. During this period I really went to the dogs, I reached rock bottom. I drank a lot and had a lot of men. I lived this kind of life for about two years until I met a man with whom I fell deeply in love. This man had so much magic that the first time he kissed me I was so electrified that I walked on air.

He was married, but despite that we had an affair which lasted eight years without his wife ever finding out. In fact at one point she accused him of being a homosexual because she knew there was something going on but couldn't pin-point it. She was frigid and frightened of sex because she didn't want to become pregnant again.

I didn't mind him living with his wife because I am not particularly possessive. I suppose that my outlook is slightly selfish because I want certain aspects of a man but not the domestic responsibility.

He was possessive though, and didn't want me to go with anyone else and for quite a long time I was faithful to him. Yet I have always wanted to be free to experience everything with anyone who tempted me.

I really came into my own with this man. He was completely uninhibited and we experimented in all sorts of ways. It was through him that I discovered my need for 'painless violence' by which I mean a need to feel that I am being dominated without involving the infliction of pain. It is difficult to capture in words but I suppose it was summed up in a recent television play when one of the characters said to the other: 'You like to be hurt without pain.'

I would dare him to do things and he would laugh while doing them. Sometimes I would tell him I loathed him and he would chase me round the house, catch me, carry me upstairs and fling me on the bed. He was very perceptive and if I was in this sort of mood he would catch on to it immediately.

With him I was able to experience total orgasm. For me an orgasm reaches a crescendo and then dies down, but it is a total experience which I feel in every part of my body. I don't really consider it an orgasm proper if it is mainly local and confined to the genital areas.

Eventually this affair ended when his wife began to become extremely neurotic. She used to grovel on the floor and plead with him not to go out. This used to upset him a great deal and began to detract from his relationship with me because he couldn't cope with the situation at home and with me. I don't usually lean on people, but at this time I was having problems with my son and I suppose that, temporarily, I looked to this man for support. One night he said: 'For God's sake, don't you lean on me too.' From that moment, the magic went out of our relationship and never fully returned. It was after this that I began to go out with other men. I would get out of bed with him and into bed with someone else within the space of hours, so I was actually destroying the relationship within myself. It had to end. When the foundations of a building begin to crumble, the building crumbles too.

I have always slept around. I don't like the word promiscuous because it has all sorts of bad connotations. The simple truth is that I like to make love. I like to find out about people and it is only after one has made love that one can get people really to talk about themselves. I think that I have probably helped a lot of people in this way. I'm not so concerned with what I get out of it. I tend to be rather altruistic about the whole thing.

The majority of men who have made love to me have been unable to bring imagination into play in their love-making. I won't tolerate this; I try to get them to see that all they are experiencing is ejaculation and that they are not at all involved. This is apparent when they reach orgasm and then they ask, 'Did you?' I want them to make a lot of noise about it. I want their experience to be inside and outside and not locked away.

I have had two opportunities when I could have had sexual encounters with other women. On neither occasion did I take advantage of this which I regret in a way because I think that one should live life to the full. If the opportunity arises again I will take advantage of it because I think that I will learn something.

Mrs. N, age 51. Occupation: housewife, London.
Education: elementary. Background: lived in poverty,
then parents immigrated from Central Europe;
unhappy childhood; married for thirty years.

I must have been about fourteen or fifteen when I first became aware of my own sexuality. Before that I was completely oblivious of sexuality either in myself or in other people. I was always lucky in getting boy-friends, in spite of the fact that I was not attractive. As a child I was almost ugly.

My parents used to quarrel a lot about money when I was young. We were very poor. I later discovered that they also quarrelled about sex. You see, my mother would nag my father about us being poor and when she was angry she would cut off his rations. I would say that my childhood was unhappy, inasmuch as I can never remember being loved; my mother didn't have time for that. I had two sisters and two brothers.

My parents never talked to me about sex. I did not even learn about menstruation from my mother. I was thirteen when I had my first period. I discovered it in the toilet at school. I must admit that I was a bit frightened, but I accepted it as I knew that it had to happen to me. I never told anyone, not even my mother. I felt that it was something you just didn't talk about. I learnt about sex through experience. The children at school didn't talk about it. I knew a little about reproduction but I knew nothing of the techniques. I never read any books on sex.

We lived in a very rough area. One day, while out walking, two boys came up to me and touched me where they shouldn't. I could have killed them. I really knew that they were trying to do something, shall we say, dirty. I think that I was about eleven when this happened and the episode upset me a great deal. I didn't tell anyone about it until recently when I told my husband. I suppose, at the time I felt ashamed that I had been touched in the so-called forbidden area.

My first sexual experience took place when I was about seventeen. Looking back and being truthful, I don't think that I loved the boy. I think that I tried to tell myself that I loved him. I was terribly curious about sex, and I knew that he wanted me. I felt guilty afterwards and I kept wondering if I was going to give away the fact that he and I had made love. The first time we had sex I didn't enjoy it. It was painful at first and I

153

don't think that I had an orgasm. At the time I didn't know what an orgasm was. This boy taught me very little about sex; he was really quite immature. When we had sex it was always illicit and clandestine. The thought that she may be caught having illicit sex is one of the biggest deterents against a woman having an orgasm; of course there is the fear of pregnancy too.

When this affair ended I met my husband. We had sex before we were married but again I was afraid of being caught. It may sound strange, but I was my husband's first woman. He desperately wanted a woman. I felt that I was giving him something rather wonderful and I know that he felt the same way. But when I look back I can see that it was all rather immature because it was sex for the sake of sex. It differed from the first experience inasmuch as I knew that he loved me. I wasn't quite sure at the time whether I loved him, but I was very fond of him, and desperately needed affection. It has always been important to me. Perhaps I was a little resentful because it occurred to me that he wanted me for sex alone. Because of the circumstances I don't think that I really enjoyed it.

Things changed for the better when we got married, because I was in my own little place. The door was shut and I knew that there would be no intruders. Soon after my marriage I achieved an orgasm. At the beginning my husband used condoms, but after I had two children I no longer trusted condoms. My husband then tried coitus interruptus. The terrible tragedy was that my husband and I were both reasonably intelligent people, and yet we did not know the rudiments of sex. We had many problems, and eventually I had a nervous breakdown. One psychiatrist I saw was absolutely certain that my condition was due to my sex-life. I was given to understand that the use of coitus interruptus was crippling me. Yet neither my husband nor I were aware of this.

The breakdown was sixteen years ago. I had been having orgasms prior to this, but there came a time when I couldn't have orgasms and I kept crying, not knowing what I was crying about. It was the psychiatrist who made me aware of the cause of my trouble. Much of it had to do with my fear of becoming pregnant again. When I had my first child it was a long birth and it was terrible. The whole procedure of childbirth was a shock to me. Then I became pregnant again when my first child was only six months old. I was very upset about it and perhaps this was my reason for suppressing orgasm.

I find it difficult to explain but I think that a woman has to feel that she is wanted. I felt that I wasn't wanted. You see, we had a lot of difficulties. When orgasm doesn't happen, your husband feels that it is his fault. Each one begins to blame the other but really it is the fault of ignorance on both sides. By the time you begin to understand the truth it is too late.

I wouldn't say that the fault lay in our not being adventurous in bed; we were always willing to try new things. My husband is much less inhibited than myself, although through him I have become less inhibited. At first I was very restrained, probably because of my upbringing. I am now wholeheartedly in agreement with the view that anything a man and woman do together by mutual consent, providing neither party is hurt, could never be considered perverted. Neither my husband nor I had this attitude when we first got married.

Before my breakdown, I had an orgasm each time we had sex. I can't really describe the sensation of orgasm except that it's a wonderful feeling. Afterwards, you can look in a mirror and even if you have a face like a tramp, you feel beautiful. Then you can go to sleep; that is the most wonderful part and something I can't do now. My husband and I still have sex but I still can't achieve an orgasm. I also suffer from insomnia and claustrophobia. I have discussed this problem over and over again, and have read numerous books on the subject, but nothing seems to help. The psychiatrist made me feel that orgasm was so important that I got to the stage where I was trying so hard that the effort itself eliminated any chance of getting there. It is a terrible thing, like chasing your own tail.

Sex for me today is not distasteful, but I know that it is not complete. However, there is always hope, I really don't know what it is stopping me having orgasms. I have listened to my psychiatrist and I have tried to do as she has told me. Even so, all this has not helped and I am beginning to think that it might be better not to make such an issue of it. Then it might just happen.

Nowadays the importance of the female orgasm tends to be over-stressed; but after all sex is not just for men. I agree that a woman should not be submissive just for the sake of the man.

Apart from orgasm, sex is pleasurable because of the intimacy. The pattern of behaviour leading up to coitus is of great importance, as is behaviour afterwards. I am quite sure that my husband and I would still love each other even if we never had sex, I sometimes think that if I had married a different kind of man, the difficulties I have had would have broken up the marriage.

My two daughters are now grown up, but they are not yet married. I have always tried to be frank with them about sex. I made a point of telling them that sex was not something to be ashamed about. I suppose that I have tried to tell them that I think it is better to sleep with someone you love rather than with just anybody. Marriage is not always necessary. I really think that it is wonderful if a couple can live together without being married. The whole set-up today is wrong. Women think that they have got to trap a man and I hate the idea. It is about time women stopped having to chase men.

I have told both my daughters about birth control. I have showed them 'the cap' that I eventually came to use. I don't need it now, of course; that is the terrible thing, we used to look forward to this time as one when all our worries would be over. Yet, I have more worry now than I ever had before.

Mrs S, age 42; Occupation: English teacher,
London. Education: private tutors. Background:
upper middle-class family in Warwickshire,
child of father's second marriage and has two
half-sisters much older than herself.

It's difficult to say exactly when I became aware of my own sexuality. I suppose I must have been about eleven or twelve. I just started to feel that there was some force in my body that hadn't been there before.

I lived on a farm so I knew about animal procreation from as far back as I can remember. However, I didn't think that this applied to people until I was older. My parents told me about sex but I never understood it. For example, I asked my mother how to tell the difference between boys and girls and she said that it was the same as the difference between dog and bitch puppies. I saw animals mating and my mother said that that was the way it was with people. I couldn't work it out at all. I could only relate it to animals. Of course, when I became older and read adult books it became more obvious to me. When I was seventeen, I began to train as a nurse. However, there were certainly large gaps in my education. I thought that it was natural that my parents didn't talk about sex in front of me. They never made me feel guilty about it but we just weren't on the same wave-length.

I was eighteen when I first had sex and I thought it was marvellous. I wasn't in the least afraid. It hurt a bit, but not as much as I had been led to believe from the various books I had read. The man was a son of a schoolfriend of my mother's. He had been a prisoner-of-war in Germany. His parents lived in South Africa and he had been repatriated to England.

He was waiting for a ship to take him back to South Africa. We were both staying with my sister and one day while she was at work, I invited him to my room. We had been out the previous evening and had discussed sex. I had said then that I would like to have sex with him. He said that he didn't want to sully me, so I told him not to be ridiculous.

I had had no experience with boys before, but he was fairly experienced. I was very much in love with him. He said he was in love with me, but it may have been a reaction after being in a prison camp without a woman for three years. My father would not permit me to marry him and one of the things at the back of my mind was that if I got pregnant that might force his hand.

I didn't have an orgasm until the third or fourth time. Orgasm is like a sort of bursting. You get wound up until you reach the point when you just burst. It only lasts for a matter of seconds, but then I feel marvellous afterwards. I think that this first sexual relationship had an effect on my subsequent sex life because it was so good.

I did count once how many men I have had sex with since then, and I think that I got up to about seventeen — it may be more now. I have spent some time abroad and so they were of different nationalities. I found that the Italians tended to be rather crude: they usually think only of their own satisfaction and getting it as quickly as possible. Norwegians are rather like that too. I suppose that occasionally Italians do think a bit about the woman, but Norwegians, never. Englishmen are terrible. Apart from my husband I have never met one who had the slightest idea of how to satisfy a woman. I had one lover from Afghanistan and one from the Lebanon. They were wonderful and very considerate. I am sure that the further East one gets, the better the men are as lovers.

I think that I have been in love about three times. I know when I am in love because I think of the other person more than I think of myself. When I'm in love with a man, it doesn't matter too much whether I have an orgasm or not because I am more interested in seeing that he has an orgasm. If I am not in love with the man, then *my* orgasm is more important and if I don't have one, I feel let down.

I didn't have orgasms with all the men I slept with. I am capable of having more than one orgasm during coitus. Three is about my limit because I then begin to get tired. I think that the American idea of the orgasm being all-important is over-stressed because the sex act should be a give-and-take between two people who are very fond of one another. I am most aroused by the reaction of my partner. If he is going out of his mind, then it sets me off.

157

I have never had an orgasm through erotic fantasy, films or literature, although these things do help to arouse me. I have masturbated during those times when sex was not available to me but I don't find it satisfactory. I can easily have an orgasm through masturbating, but I always feel rather let down afterwards. Orgasm really is a physical sensation plus the thoughts it triggers off. At times when I am having sex, I fantasise. Sometimes it is almost a slave fantasy and sometimes I imagine that I am a girl from a South Italian village, where morality is strong, and that I have just got married and have been released from this strict code. However, I have no great need to fantasise: I just do it occasionally.

Whipping and caning I dislike. I had a lover once who used to beat me with a collection of twigs which he used to get from the garden. I didn't particularly like it . . . but if it amused him, okay! The only thing that men have expected me to do which I find distasteful is fellatio. I have done it when I have been very fond of the man.

In England I find that the men are not really aware of the physical and psychological needs of a woman. In the East the men are far more aware that a woman needs arousing. They are much more patient and willing to try to arouse her and take a great interest in her reactions.

I think that a woman needs very much to be caressed before she can become really aroused. She definitely needs to feel that the man has some affection for her. On the practical side, she needs somewhere comfortable to make love. I think that it is awful doing it in a car because one gets all tied up with the gears.

Essentially, the role of a woman is to give pleasure to a man. I get my pleasure from giving pleasure to someone else. This isn't meant in the Victorian sense at all, because I don't see how a woman can give pleasure to a man by being passive. I don't think that I was ever taught to make love. I just knew from the beginning and improved with practice.

I have always been able to talk to men about sex, except if the man is very inhibited. That tends to inhibit me because I am always afraid of embarrassing him. I never know what to say to Englishmen because they are embarrassed easily. I suppose that my liberated attitude towards sex stems from the fact that I have always been rather independent. I was a nurse during the latter part of the War and this gives one a sort of medical attitude.

If I had children, I would try to gear their minds towards thinking that sex is a thing to be enjoyed but that it is not a good idea to go to bed with just everybody. I suppose that I could have done without one or two of the men I've slept with, but on the other hand I don't think that I have slept with too many because I gained valuable experience.

However, I have now come to the point where I don't want to sleep with anyone except the man I am living with. I met him through a personal advert in a newspaper. I had been abroad for four years and when I returned, I found it difficult to make men friends in London. I had a married lover but I could see that this wasn't going to work out, so I began to answer two advertisements every week. I met lots of men, some of whom were nice, some of whom were not, and among them is the man I am now living with, whom I consider as my husband.

He is married at present, but he is getting a divorce. He met his wife the same way he met me. We went out occasionally; then he wrote saying that he was getting married. I heard no more from him for about nine or ten months. One day he telephoned and asked me out to dinner. His marriage apparently hadn't worked out.

A lot of the men whose adverts I answered expected me to have sex with them, but I never had sex with anyone the first time I went out with them. I would certainly advise lonely women to answer these adverts, because after all, one can sort the wheat from the chaff, although you do get a lot of chaff!

As I mentioned, I did have a lover who was married. I felt that he would always have sex outside his marriage and that his wife knew this. I thought that as long as I didn't break up the marriage it was all right. At the moment, I am faithful to my 'husband' and this means a lot to me. Of course it is easy for me to say this because at present I don't know anyone else I would want to have sex with. I feel that I have knocked about quite a lot and now I want to settle down with one person. If my husband was unfaithful to me, I would rather not know about it, but, on the other hand, if he was tired of me I would far rather he went out now and then with other women, than leave me completely. I suppose that if he wasn't tired of me and just wanted sex with another woman occasionally, I could come to accept this.

I agree with the view that anything a man and a woman do together, by mutual consent, providing it hurts neither partner, can never be considered perverted. Actually my husband and I just like straightforward sex with him on top and me underneath. We have tried other ways but we enjoy the so-called missionary position so much that we may as well get on with it.

Once, while living in France, I did have an affair with a woman, and that was because I was terrified of becoming pregnant. I had had a nasty scare in Norway. I was having an affair with a Norwegian and there is one thing that Norwegian men are not keen on and that is contraception, chiefly because it costs money. They use coitus interruptus and I don't think that they are very good at that either.

This scare turned me off sex with men for a long time. I met my girlfriend in a café in Paris which is specially for women. I thought that I would like a girlfriend because I needed sex, but at the same time I didn't want a man. I knew that there were such cafés in Paris so I went along to one. However, sex with a woman is much less complete than sex with a man, specially if one of the women is trying to be a man, which was the case with my girlfriend. She became terribly possessive and jealous about my relationships with other people, men or women. I think that I could still be attracted to another woman, but it would worry me because I would feel that I was being unfaithful to my husband.

After this affair, I decided to fit myself out with a contraceptive cap because I knew that my sex had to be with a man. Since then, I have used the Pill, but this was bad for my health so now I am fitted with an intra-uterine device.

Miss Q, age 21. Occupation: typist, Lincolnshire.
Education: grammar school.
Background:
only child of middle-class parents.

I must have been a particularly stupid child because until I was about eight years old it never occurred to me that a conspiracy was afoot to prevent me from knowing certain things. I woke up to this when other children began to shake my faith in the story of the stork.

Suddenly, it became tremendously important to me to know where I came from. My questions were answered with more stork tales, or else mutterings about gooseberry bushes. I knew all this wasn't true and went through a stage when I thought that my parents believed it. I was worried that I knew something they didn't. I thought that they really had found me under a gooseberry bush and adopted me. I went through this period of thinking that I was adopted and not knowing whether or not to tell my parents that babies really didn't just grow under bushes. I think that if I had actually known at the time where babies did come from I would have gone to my parents with the view of telling them something I thought they didn't know.

However, I soon found out. My initiation into sex came when a boy a

160

few years older asked me if I knew what 'spunk' was. I pretended to know because I didn't want him to think I was ignorant. Of course, I hadn't the faintest idea what he was talking about, except I had this exciting feeling that it was all rather dark and forbidden territory. He then proceeded to tell me a dirty joke about a honeymoon couple, which even to this day I can't recall without distaste. Gradually I began to piece it all together and got to the stage of playing around with my friends. I had one particular friend, a boy whom I thought I would marry when I grew up. One day he and another girl and myself were in a shed and we had all removed our underwear. I made him put his penis in me. As far as I remember I enjoyed it all tremendously, despite the fact that I was only about seven or eight years old. There I was having a wonderful time when my father came in. I don't think I will ever be able to describe how I felt. I wanted to be sick with guilt. He was very calm and ordered me into the house. He never mentioned the incident, but the next morning my mother raised hell. She didn't shout at me, she just made me feel that I had committed original sin. She went on about promising not to tell my headmistress at school and my aunty and uncles, but said if she caught me doing it again she would have to tell them. I got the impression that anyone who knew what I had been doing would never speak to me again because they would think me such a dreadful person.

I cried and cried and begged forgiveness, which she graciously granted. But things were never the same again. I felt dirty and soiled and nothing could remove it. At the same time I began to feel this compulsive attraction towards boys. I adored kissing boys and wanted to be the centre of attraction.

When I was a little older I developed my first real crush. I was crazy about this boy. I had always indulged in fantasies about boys and current heroes such as television cowboys, but after I met him I spent all my days in a fantasy world. Most of my fantasies were sexual, but in a naive sort of way, feeling and kissing and things like that. They were also full of compliments and flattery, like him telling me I was pretty.

The truth was that I wasn't at all pretty and suffered agonies because of it. For about two years I tortured myself over this boy. He was older than me and had lots of very sophisticated girl friends. He was sweet to me in a brotherly sort of way. I remember once that he danced with me and I felt quite weak. My face was burning and I was wobbly at the knees, as well as being horribly embarrassed at not being able to dance well.

During this time I made friends with a crowd of girls much older than myself. I think that they liked me because I was cute. I was far too intelligent for my age and this made me appear rather old-fashioned and amusing.

These girls were all about fifteen while I was only twelve. They were all having sex with lots of different boys and I envied them enormously. I had long drawn out petting sessions with some of these boys, which usually consisted of my masturbating them to orgasm. I found it all extremely exciting, mainly because of the furtiveness and because it awakened all kinds of feelings within me which I had only suspected were there.

Eventually of course I was deflowered. He was a handsome guy, about six years older than me. I felt let down by the whole thing. It was painful and uncomfortable. He fumbled and mauled me before leaving me to walk home alone.

However, from then on there was no stopping me. I was so promiscuous that it frightens me to think about what the consequences could have been. It was really quite tragic because I didn't know what the hell I was doing . . . except that I wasn't supposed to be doing it.

There was one boy whom I grew very fond of. He was my most regular partner. In fact, I am sure that if he hadn't messed about with other girls I would never have been promiscuous and would have been quite happy to have been with him. I used to get quite upset when I saw him with other girls. My affection for him was sincere and lasted for a long time. However, I seemed to calm down for a while and things were going along at an even keel. It was the year of my 'O' level exams and I began to think that I was really getting myself sorted out. Then I met C.

This was probably the most fatal thing which has ever happened to me. The beginning of my affair with C. was like a fairy tale. We went for long walks in the country and talked until our heads were empty. I don't think that I had ever opened up to another human being the way I opened up to him, neither had I felt so devoted to anyone.

The first time we made love I thought that I was going to die there and then because that was what life was all about and there wasn't much else to touch beyond it. I had never had an orgasm before. In fact for a while I went on having orgasms without knowing what they were. As far as I was concerned it was a magical experience which was induced by means of his spell upon me.

It's impossible to describe adequately, words are soiled by all sorts of connotations and this feeling is so pure. It is as if you are filled with the essence which is in all living things; as if the spirit of all that has lived, does live or will ever live passes through you. It is an affirmation that you are holy.

162

In a way I suppose that I felt guilty about loving him so much. At that age there is this big parent thing of their expecting you to have a career and all the mass media stuff which is churned out about young love being very lovely but totally unreal. I felt that no one understood the way I loved him, not even him. It was a huge and magnificent load to carry around without being able to communicate it to anyone. I felt that if I tried to tell someone they would laugh and say that no one could possibly love another human being that much, let alone a fifteen-year-old school-girl who 'couldn't possibly know her own mind anyway'.

I badly wanted to tell my mother. I wanted her to say that she was glad I could love that intensely. I wanted her to understand more than anyone, but I realised from her attitude that she couldn't. She used to get quite annoyed about C. and I taking long walks hand in hand and things like that. I don't think that it bothered her from a moral point of view; it was just that she hadn't planned anything like that happening until I had gone to university and got all the desirable bits of paper.

It was inevitable that I had to come back down to earth. In spite of being older than me he was still quite young and I think that my emotional high frightened him. He wasn't ready for such an intense relationship. Anyway the whole thing blew up and I went crazy. I ran away in desperation and spent a miserable two months in a large city, which didn't really help me because all I could think about was getting back and seeing him again.

I was allowed to stay as long as I did on the understanding that I would go back, which I did. Then came a dreadful period when C. and I fell in and out of bed without really getting anywhere. I was so unhappy that it didn't take much for he and my mother to persuade me to leave town with the idea of starting afresh. I went off not quite knowing where I was going or why. It was three months before I went home again and then it was on the understanding that C. wouldn't be around. However, he was and the whole thing started again. Looking back, I can see that I wasn't being weak by going to bed with him whenever I went home for a visit, because after all I had been used to having sex regularly and suddenly it wasn't there. I must have been terribly frustrated, but didn't realise it at the time.

About a year later he disappeared for a long while. I had lots of boyfriends, none of whom I wanted. But I had to go on trying. I desperately needed someone to love. I'd start out on a relationship and think 'Yes, this will be alright.' But when it came to the crunch I somehow could not permit myself to go all the way.

No doubt, most of the mental suffering was due to the fact that I wasn't having sex. I am convinced that being deprived of sex after having had a full sex-life can throw anyone. On the other hand, I learnt a great deal about myself and how to cope with my own desires. When you are messed up inside, you tend to go into things such as literature and philosophy as an attempt to sort yourself out and on the way you stumble across all sorts of truths. You discover people with vision, you begin to have visions of your own and realise the futility of despair.

I don't claim even now to have worked out why during this time I could meet men whom I found attractive sexually, intellectually and emotionally and yet have been incapable of making love to them. It began to worry me a great deal because I thought that it reflected an inadequacy within myself.

I began to think that I was frigid, but at the same time I knew my behaviour with people in general was not that of a frigid woman.

Eventually, I prepared myself for another try. I had sex with a boy whom I found physically attractive, but with whom I had no common ground. It was disastrous. His approach wasn't exactly imaginative and I honestly felt that he never really wanted me anyway — that it was just a matter of convenience. I never came anywhere near to orgasm. The whole scene just made me even more convinced that something was seriously wrong.

A few months later C. reappeared. As soon as I saw him I realised that I was far from frigid. I merely abandoned myself to what was to be. I tried not to think about the briefness of our times together. After a while we fell into a more normal relationship, in a way which was natural without being habitual. There is no direction in our relationship, which seems to bother a lot of people, but that's the only way it can work.

Sometimes I think in terms of having children and a home. But I have come to accept that I will probably never have these things. There are black periods when this bothers me a great deal but I feel that I have to be realistic. It would be better if I was the sort of person who could think — well, I'll marry someone else for all that and finish up quite happy, but I know that I can't.

The ideal solution for us would be for me to be able to go ahead and have a child and at the same time to be self-sufficient, but that is unrealistic in a society geared to the family concept. The child would suffer and that would be unjust, although it makes me angry that this has to be and that society by virtue of its format imposes these strict limitations.

I would be quite willing to go through with it, and perhaps the child would be happy enough if I were capable of teaching him to cope successfully with a hostile environment. It would depend so much on the nature of the child. He could turn out to be so sensitive as to be naturally vulnerable. I am not sure that I would be morally right in taking such a risk.

As a woman I think I have a great responsibility in not perpetuating things which have led to a great deal of suffering in the past. I think that if, as a woman, you are constantly developing as a person you have a great deal more to offer than the facilities of your womb for procreating the species. However, there does seem to be this deeply rooted need for a child. The conflict I have not yet resolved is apparent in the word 'need'. I am not sure whether or not for me to have a child would be just an act of selfishness.

Index